Planting Healthy Growing Churches

The Key To Transforming People, Cities & Nations

Dr. George S. Hill

Bradley T. Dewar

Victory International Publishing

VIP

SPECIAL THANKS:

Thank you to Dr. Hazel Hill for her contribution and consultation on the topic of church planters wives.

Thank you to Juliet Rainy-Brown and Nora Forsey for their efforts in proofreading.

Thank you to Douglas Binet for interior layout and cover design.

Table of Contents:

Introduction

Christianity is a group activity. Salvation is indeed personal but Christianity is not. This has always been the truth and is still true today despite the prevailing culture of individualism and personal isolationism. When people are born again they are born into the family of God and spend the remainder of eternity in the family. Indeed God's plan to bring believers to spiritual maturity and character can only take place within the context of committed, long-term relationships with other people.

That means that planting churches is no optional activity. It forms the heart and soul of the Great Commission. It is the raison d'etre of the church and its primary occupation. All other activities of Christian ministry are incidental to the formation and multiplication of local churches.

And in today's highly mobile and multi-cultural social mix it requires an ever increasing diversity of local churches to effectively reach and disciple people from every segment of society.

This rapidly shifting social landscape has put the traditional church in the position of having to either change or die. Some indeed would rather die than change. But there is a growing number within the church that are willing to step out of the boat of conventionalism and walk on the waters of church planting in response to the call of the Lord. As a result we are experiencing a world-wide movement of modern day church planting.

New churches infuse the whole body of Christ with new excitement, new ideas, new frontiers of ministry and new people. New churches produce new leaders which are desperately needed today. In fact, new churches are vital to the health and continued growth of the whole church.

However, like many other worthwhile things, church planting is easier said than done. Or in other words, if it was easy – everybody would be doing it. In fact, it requires a special set of skills and a special kind of teamwork. Church planters know what it means to live by faith and to see God respond to their faith in practical and tangible ways.

But since it is God's mission and God's call, God generously supplies the resources, the power, and the direction that it takes.

This book is arranged in three main sections: preparation before planting, the planting process, and what to do after the new church is launched. It is a result of our own experiences gained in planting churches ourselves and coaching many others. Although it may serve as a starting place, it is our hope that it may inspire others to go far beyond what we have done and pioneer whole new approaches to expanding the Kingdom through the planting of thousands of vibrant new churches.

Bradley T. Dewar

Forward:

A First Generational Pioneer Movement

Victory Churches is a first generational pioneer movement that is rapidly expanding all around the world. It is an apostolic, prophetic, church planting/growth movement that, in it's first 20 years, enjoyed an average annual growth rate of 20 – 25%.

We thank God for the past and all that has been accomplished through His grace and favor. Our past gives us tremendous hope for the future, because if God can do what He has done with the little He had to work with yesterday, imagine what He can do in the future with what we have now!

As we look to the future we can see a world full of opportunities for those who are totally committed to Christ and willing to serve. Jesus Himself has declared:

> *The harvest truly is plentiful, but the laborers are few. Therefore pray the Lord of the harvest to send out laborers into His harvest. (Matt 9:37-38)*

> *Lift up your eyes and look at the fields, for they are already white for harvest!* (John 4:35)

It Is Harvest Time!

Charles Finney said, "Revival is no more miraculous than a crop of wheat."

> *I planted, Apollos watered, but God gave the increase. (1 Cor 3:6)*

A great future doesn't just happen anymore than a good garden just happens. If you are not thinking, planning and preparing for the future, you end up living in the past. The future belongs to those who are willing to invest in it.

We must have a mindset of foresight.

> *"A prudent man foresees the evil and hides himself, but the simple pass on and are punished"* (Prov 22:3).

We must think at least two years ahead, otherwise we will always be in a crisis, survival, maintenance mode, instead of an aggressive, possessing-the-land mode.

Like the children of Issachar, we have seen where things were going and have acted accordingly (1 Chron 12:32). To maintain this position, we must constantly be building for the future. This means we must have foreknowledge, forethought, foresight, insight, a prophetic edge, and pioneering spirit.

We must invest in the future now. People don't sacrifice anything for today, but if they can catch a glimpse of what the future could look like, they would be willing to sacrifice something small today for something gigantic tomorrow. It's the principle of delayed gratification. We pay now and play later.

The future is worth fighting for. The battle is not over your past or your present; it's over your future. Destroy the author and the book will never be written; destroy the musician and the song will never be sung. We must continue to be pioneers: pioneer churches and pioneer pastors, leaders and people.

Every generation needs a first generational pioneer movement. Settlers are quite happy to stay and maintain what already exists; but pioneers are always seeking to go beyond the present boundaries. There is more to Christianity, to Church, to life, to the Holy Spirit and the power of God than we have ever experienced. And we are going after it!

> *And they went out and preached everywhere, the Lord working with them and confirming the word through the accompanying signs.*
> - (Mark 16:20)

God's plan to transform nations is in the planting and building of enough Jesus-loving, Bible-believing, Holy Spirit-filled, soul-winning, New Testament type churches.

The biggest and longest lasting revivals that have ever taken place were church planting movements. The Methodists were a church planting movement with John Wesley as the apostolic leader. He had a systematic plan on how to plant churches all around the world.

Then the Pentecostal churches came along at a later date. They didn't have a plan. It just happened spontaneously by the Holy Spirit.

I believe the last great move of God will encompass both the Methodist and the Pentecostal movements. It will be a move that has an aggressive, strategic plan to plant churches all around the world, together with a spontaneous move of the Holy Spirit.

My confidence is that as you read this book you will sense the heartbeat of God and be thrust forth into Holy Spirit-directed and empowered service.

It's time for another Great Awakening! It's time to rise up and transform our communities and our nations by being co-laborers with Jesus Christ in the exciting work of building His Church (Matthew 16:18). It's time for the militant, miraculous and triumphant church to arise and be about the Father's business! Let's do it big; let's do it good; and let's do it together!

Dr. George S. Hill

SECTION 1
Church Planting In The 21st Century

1.1 HISTORICAL TRENDS IN CHURCH PLANTING

The New Testament was written during an aggressive church planting move. It was an infectious social revolution that began in Jerusalem following the ascension of Christ, and eventually spread to the farthest reaches of the Roman Empire. In fact, some of the churches that were established in that first wave of expansion are still in operation today!

In those days, nobody thought to differentiate church planting from evangelism. They had a mandate to spread the news of salvation, and assumed that the formation of churches would be the natural outcome. Fanning out from Jerusalem, and later Antioch, the early apostles had a clear mission: preach the Gospel everywhere and establish cells of converts for ongoing discipleship and training. In fact, we could say that without church planting - evangelism, in and of itself, can quickly become misguided and ineffective. When we study Jesus' 'evangelistic' passages it becomes clear that he never intended his followers to simple go and preach – but to go and make disciples.

Making disciples implies several things:

- ✓ A process of time. Converts can be born in a single Gospel encounter, but no disciple is made overnight.

- ✓ It implies a deliberate, systematic approach. Discipline, the root of discipleship, is never a haphazard thing. It must be thorough, comprehensive, and sensibly ordered.

- ✓ It assumes that not only are there disciples being made, but that someone is discipling them. This necessitates teachers, leaders, and spiritual mentors.

- ✓ And it infers that all of this takes place as a group activity.

There may be many valid definitions of the church – but none better than this. It's a long term approach to turning converts into growing servants of God through committed relationship with spiritual leaders. The New Testament writers may have called it 'gathering together', but they were forming churches from day one.

And so the history of the expansion and development of Christianity is also the story of church planting. Wave after wave and nation after nation. The Mediterranean region is littered with the historic ruins of church structures that marked their progress. Five hundred years later it surged across Europe, cluttering the continent with cathedral spires. The tide next flowed to the Orient and then to the New world – all resulting in thousands upon thousands of local churches. Without the establishment of local churches there would have been no way to gauge either the number of converts or the ultimate impact on society. Without church planting there would be no lasting legacy to shape our collective history.

The Protestant movement was germinated in the circles of theological debate, but became an historical reality only when protestant churches were planted across northern Europe and then around the world. It was the formation of thousands of local churches in America and Canada that provided much of the impetus and the foundation for these two great modern day democracies.

During the last 150 years the prevalence of secularism, fuelled by evolutionary theory and rapid scientific advances, all but brought an end to the growth of the church in the West, let alone the planting of new churches. But this shift in thinking has been challenged in more recent years by the phenomenal growth of Christianity in Africa, Asia, and South America. This has stirred North American church leaders to once again take the offensive. It is safe to say that the future story of the church will also be tracked by the planting of new churches.

1.2 CONTEMPORARY FACTORS

A couple of major trends impact upon church planting in North America today. The first is immigration. A tide of third world migration is taking place in first-world nations today that, by all indications, is only going to intensify going forward. Economical means of transportation, unprecedented availability of global information, and exploding population rates in developing nations are pushing immigration quotas to record levels. Coastal cities are already flooded with newcomers. In destination cities like Toronto virtually one out of two people were born outside of Canada. Even landlocked cities in the mid-west are now home to a rapidly burgeoning shift in cultural diversity.

This is a tremendous opportunity for the planting of new churches! Although immigrant people bring their culture and religious background with them, they tend to arrive in their new country with a very open mind and a readiness to adapt to their new society. Many, in fact, arrive with a much stronger Christian orientation than the secularized peoples amongst whom they settle. This means that new churches will tend to have a much higher proportion of ethnic minorities. Church programs and outreaches have to reflect this multi-cultural reality.

The second major social trend at work today is urbanization. When we Baby-Boomers were born about one third of the world's population lived in a major city. Today roughly 50% are city-dwellers. By the time we celebrate our 85th birthdays over two thirds will live in a city. And not just any city – this massive migration of human beings is rapidly turning yesterday's urbanizations of one million into sprawling slum cities of twenty and thirty million people. This means that as church planters we can no longer envision a nice rural parish as our goal. The mission field of the 21st century is the mega-city.

The challenges faced here are very different from the rural-based mentality that many Christians have carried over from past generations. The new paradigm for many will be overwhelming poverty. Trapped in a desperate cycle of overloaded economies and out-dated infrastructures, millions will spend their lives in slum neighbourhoods with little hope of getting out. The church must go in.

For those who can afford to live uptown, the exorbitant cost of living keeps them so busy running the rat race that it's hard for churches to get a foothold. The larger the city, the more people tend to hide behind the security of anonymity and evade personal commitments. With so much going on all around, all the time – it's hard for new churches to even get noticed in the mega-city.

Planting churches here requires some mega-thinking, mega-teamwork, and some mega-faith. But God loves cities! Perhaps this is the real message of the prophet Jonah.

Mega-cities are like the magnetic core of a nation, drawing all the people, finances, and attention to themselves. But as such, they are often the keys to changing whole nations. Win the city – win the nation! Remember, the Bible may begin in a garden, but it ends in a city!

In order to meet this massive challenge the world needs thousands and thousands of vibrant new, innovative types of churches. We will also need that many more senior leaders, planting team members, and visionary organizations to send and support them. Never has there been a greater need and a greater opportunity to go forth and "do exploits" for God than there is in our generation. The future belongs to those who can rapidly and consistently mobilize capable new leaders.

There Is A Need

In order to effectively evangelize an area, it takes one good church for every 2,000 people. One church growth expert says that, "The greatest evangelistic methodology under heaven is the planting of new churches." The local church and having enough good local churches is God's plan to transform nations. The local church is not one of God's optional programs—it's His only program. Jesus said, "I will build my church and the gates of Hades shall not prevail against it" (Matthew 18:16). This is a guarantee of success, if we work together with Jesus to build His church the way He says we should build it.

The United Nations estimates that by the year 2050 the world's population will increase to 12 billion. That means there will be approximately twice as many people on the earth as there were at the turn of the century. Based on the formula of one good church for every 2,000 people, the Church will need to plant another three million churches by the year 2050 just to keep up with the population growth!

Just as the future of the human race is dependent upon new babies being birthed into this world, so the future of the Church is dependent upon the planting of fresh, new, vibrant churches.

The Church Needs To Release Ministry

The job of the five-fold ministry is to equip and release people into ministry (Ephesians 4:11-13). Without a church planting vision, we train people to be either frustrated or to split churches. If we don't release people, they can become discouraged and critical, or even rebellious. Too many trained leaders, all with the same gifting, all in one church, can become like a planting pot with too many plants in it. The plants become root-bound. The roots begin to choke each other.

There is just not enough room for growth. Proverbs 11:24-25 says:

> *"There is one who scatters, yet increases more; and there is one who withholds more than is right, but it leads to poverty".*

The generous soul will be made rich and he who waters will also be watered himself.

If a local church does not plan to plant churches, it will probably end up doing so anyway. It's just that it will be done the wrong way! The Message Bible version says,

> *"The world of the generous gets larger and larger, the world of the stingy gets smaller and smaller."*

A New Church Gives New Hope

As the last generation walked away from the church of their parents they carried a lot of cynicism and disillusionment with them. They saw no point in participating in a dead, hypocritical church. Outside of a wedding or a funeral, many have never been back to church since. But a new church gives new hope. For many who have been hurt and disappointed or rejected by existing churches for various reasons, it gives the possibility of a new start.

A New Church Raises The Standard

A new church in the community raises the standard in many of the existing churches; much like a new restaurant raises the standard of the other existing restaurants. If you only have one good restaurant in an area, it is not too long before the prices increase, the portions get smaller, and the service begins to deteriorate. But, when a new exciting restaurant comes into town offering special meals at special prices, served by the best waiters and waitresses, the old restaurant had better smarten up, or it will lose its customers.

This process may not be comfortable for existing churches, but in the end it is tremendously beneficial to them and their own growth prospects.

One Size Does Not Fit All

There is a prevailing mindset among evangelical Christians that bigger is always better. Hence the mega-church trend in the last 20 years or so. Building a mega-church is widely seen as the ultimate measure of success.

This typically means a single church with attendance counted in thousands that boasts the resources to be everything to everybody. And although there are indeed many benefits of a large church, it does not suit everyone. For example, those who just prefer a smaller more neighbourhood sized church! Nor does it serve the development of five-fold leaders as effectively as does a smaller church. Not everyone will respond well to the same individual leader. That is why God designated a multiplicity of leadership gifts in the church. Only exposure to a wider variety of these anointings can activate God's leadership call in a wider variety of people.

As we examine the church plants in the book of Acts, we discover several principles that will help us in our own church planting endeavours.

Jerusalem - Acts 2:37-47

Jesus' first church plant took place in Jerusalem. I think it's worth noting that the Lord only let Peter have a one-day crusade in order to get this church off the ground. Did you ever wonder why they only continued the meeting for one day, when 3,000 people were saved in that short a time? Most of us would have extended the meeting, and stayed as long as we could, once we saw that kind of success!

I believe that Jesus was planting His church responsibly. It would have been irresponsible for Jesus to let Peter have a seven-day crusade and keep on winning souls. He only had a 120 leaders. If any more people had been saved, this new church would not have been able to handle it. John Wesley makes this point in a quotation from his own Journal (1703-1791):

I was more convinced than ever before that the preaching like an Apostle, without joining together those that are awakened and training them up in the ways of God is only begetting children for the murderer. How much preaching has there been for these twenty years all over Pembrokeshire! (Wales) But no regular societies, no discipline, no order or connection; and the consequences are that nine out of ten of the once awakened are now faster asleep than ever.

A lot of times we see evangelists go into a third-world nation to hold a crusade. They advertise the meetings and 30,000 people come forward to get saved. What they aren't telling you is that many of these same people were saved in someone else's meeting two years earlier. But the evangelist gets great pictures for his magazine of thousands coming to the Lord and then he goes home. That's just irresponsible. We need to have adequate follow up and discipleship. I am glad to say that today many evangelists are now beginning to work together with apostolic leaders and churches in the area and the harvest is being conserved.

When Jesus planted His church, He made sure He had adequate leaders. Actually, He didn't have quite enough, according to the Exodus 18 principle. In order to have enough leaders, He would have needed 300 "leaders of tens," 60 "leaders of fifties," 30 "leaders of hundreds," three "leaders of thousands," and one "leader of 3,000". That comes to 394 leaders in all. But remember, the 120 were hand-picked and personally mentored by Jesus the wise Master Builder.

We need to follow Jesus' example and be responsible. We have started many churches with over 200 people in the opening service, but before we did that we made sure we were fully prepared to be able to follow-up on that many people. Otherwise we would have been acting negligently. There is much more to this than just getting two or three hundred people together for a service.

You have to have all of the other vital elements in place as well.

When we started our first church in Toronto, Canada, we had 366 people show up for the first Sunday service. But we did it responsibly. Three months in advance we sent a team of five-fold ministers including four pastoral leaders, their wives and five Bible College interns into the area where we wanted our church. Then when we had a good turnout we were able to follow up on them. You cannot build a house bigger than its foundation. When a church outgrows its foundation, it is in trouble. Apostles and prophets are foundation specialists, ensuring healthy, sustainable growth (Eph 2:20).

Samaria - Acts 8:1-25

In Acts 1:8 Jesus gave the disciples a plan to reach the world. They were to start in Jerusalem. Then, they were to branch out into Judea. From Judea they were to reach out into Samaria.

But by Acts 8 they still hadn't moved out of Jerusalem. Everything was in place in the church but no one was reaching the regions beyond Jerusalem. Jesus didn't give the disciples the power for just Jerusalem; He equipped them to reach out to the entire world! It wasn't until persecution occurred that the Christians were forcibly scattered throughout Judea and Samaria.

Some of the things you struggle with are often the very things that push you into the will of God. Sometimes things go wrong to make you more right. Here the persecution pushed them into the very thing that God had commanded them to do. Many people tend to settle for comfort and pleasure rather than growth, change and advancement. However, God knows how to stir up the nest and mobilize His people.

The key thing with the Samaritan church was their cultural affinity to the Jewish people. It is rare that God picks us up and drops us into the middle of a completely foreign environment. Instead he works at gradually enlarging our 'measure of rule'. New churches will typically have better success reaching family and friends, and those within our own relational circle. Then he connects us to our neighbours and those in similar neighbourhoods until we finally reach the other side of town – but we are standing on a firm relational foundation when we do.

Antioch - Acts 11:19-30

Here we see the birthing of the church at Antioch. The church in Jerusalem sent Barnabas to Antioch. He was sent, and he went. It doesn't say the Holy Spirit led him. Those in authority in the church in Jerusalem sent Barnabas to plant the church in Antioch and then stay on to pastor the people. This was the church that eventually became the greatest missionary sending church of the first century.

In Acts 13 we see five of the church's leaders ministering to the Lord and fasting; and the Spirit of God gave them fresh direction.

Now in the church that was at Antioch there were certain prophets and teachers: Barnabas, Simeon who was called Niger, Lucius of Cyrene, Manaen who had been brought up with Herod the tetrarch, and Saul. As they ministered to the Lord and fasted, the Holy Spirit said,

> "Now separate to Me Barnabas and Saul for the work to which I have called them." (Acts 13:1-2.)

The word of the Lord was received and acted upon immediately; because this church had a spirit of faith and a releasing spirit.

Barnabas and Saul were released into the ministry God had for them, and the church grew on without them.

This openness to the leading of the Holy Spirit came as a result of a certain spiritual climate in the church.

Their commitment to prayer probably included a vibrant worship life, since the two often go hand-in-hand.

But the real strength of the Antioch church was its understanding of five-fold ministry. The passage above indicates the ordinary operation of prophets and teachers in their meetings. Acts 15 also mentions Judas and Silas being prophets at Antioch. After this commissioning, both Paul and Barnabus were designated as apostles.

It would seem that their success in planting churches far and wide around the northern shores of the Mediterranean was at least partially a result of placing leaders according to their five-fold gifting: pastors and teachers tending the flock at home, prophets contributing guidance at critical decision-points, and apostles planting new churches.

Macedonia - Acts 16:5-15; 25-31

The first New Testament church was birthed in Jerusalem. Then the Antioch church was raised up with a heart and passion to reach the world. It was from Antioch that Paul sought to go into Asia, but the Holy Spirit forbade him (Acts 16:6-7).

It's interesting that three chapters later in Acts 19, Paul went into the very same place that God wouldn't let him go earlier. Just because God didn't allow you to go somewhere a few years ago doesn't necessarily mean that He doesn't want you to go there now. Sometimes we don't get a green light because the timing isn't right.

In Paul's case the timing wasn't right. So he sought the Lord's direction. As he prayed and sought God he had a vision of a man from Macedonia saying, "Come over to Macedonia and help us" (Acts 16:10). As soon as Paul knew God's leading he immediately obeyed. Today's obedience positions us for tomorrow's breakthroughs and revivals.

Timing is crucial for new churches to succeed. It must be the right time for the key leader, the right time for the core group, and the right time for the target community.

When Paul arrived in Macedonia, he found a group of people who were praying for someone to come there and help them. We often find this identical situation - a group of people in a city praying for God to move or asking God to help them. Eventually they either called us or we found them and a new church was planted. How exciting it is following Jesus and being led by the Holy Spirit!

Some people prefer to play it so safe. But they tend to remain spiritually dormant. They never do anything for God. It's better to step out on the water and be in a position where God might have to come and save you, than to play it safe and never experience God's power. Someone said, "If you ever achieve ultimate security you will also achieve ultimate boredom." What good is life if you don't live it! When is the last time you did something for the first time?

Church planters are risk takers! They will go where others won't go, and do what others won't do. As a result, their lives brim with excitement and rewards. William Carey, the great missionary to India said: "Attempt great things for God, expect great things from God."

Thessalonica And Corinth - Acts 17:1-10; 18:1-11

This was an interesting church plant. Paul and his team were only in Thessalonica for three weeks. This church was birthed in the same way Paul planted several of his churches. He would go into the Synagogue on the Sabbath day and teach from the Scriptures how the crucified and resurrected Christ was the Jewish Messiah. The acceptance or rejection of the Gospel message does cause a separation between the believers and the unbelievers. The group that believed in Jesus were excommunicated from the Synagogue, and established fellowship and support groups which became churches. The group that didn't believe frequently wanted to stone Paul, usually forcing him to leave town in a hurry! That's why Paul only stayed a few weeks in Thessalonica. Church planters may not be the most popular people in town.

Why? Because they can be a threat to those steeped in religion and to those who are in error, or to those who are territorial and are perhaps afraid to lose part of their congregation.

Eventually Paul began to wonder how the church was doing; so he sent Timothy to Thessalonica. When Timothy arrived, he found a thriving work for God. Paul stayed different lengths of time in different places: three weeks in Thessalonica, 18 months in Corinth, and three years in Ephesus.

It just depended on what needed to be done and then Paul, remaining sensitive and obedient to God's will and timing, would leave when his part of the job was complete.

When you're planting a church, you can't say that you're going to be there for a specific period of time. It will vary from church plant to church plant. Every place you go into, you should go with the attitude that you'll be there as long as it takes. When it's time to leave, leave in a responsible fashion. No one should leave a church before they have trained or arranged responsible leadership to turn the church over to. It's a crime for someone to start a church, and then leave because they get frustrated. The sheep are scattered and people get hurt. It makes it difficult for God to bless that person in the next place.

On the other hand there is often more damage done by pastors staying too long than pastors leaving too soon. Church planters stay too long because of one of two reasons: The first being a sense of security. They think to themselves: "I have built this church to the place where I can now receive a decent salary and I want to enjoy the security for a while. Besides, I love these people and don't want to leave them." The second reason for a church planter staying too long is a sense of duty: "I have planted this church and now it's time for me to move on but there is no one to replace me." Of course the answer to this is to train a successor.

Within the fellowship of our Victory Churches we help church planters to recognize when their time is up and help them to leave while the people still love them. We do this by helping them find a replacement pastor so they can fulfill their responsibility. Then we help them financially by paying their salary and supporting them financially in the next church plant where necessary. This provides security for them and their family as they move to their next assignment without having to worry about finances.

Your destiny is made up of a series of God given assignments. Every assignment fulfilled prepares you for the next one. The most important thing is to finish well; this may mean staying somewhere longer than you really want. If you don't finish well, it doesn't matter how many good things you did, people remember how you finished. Finish well and finish responsibly.

Ephesus - Acts 19:1-26

In this church we see the process, the principles, and the results of revival. We see Paul, the wise master builder, at work. This church began with a small group of men who were praying. Paul asked whether they had received the Holy Spirit, and they replied, "We have not so much as heard whether there is a Holy Spirit." Then Paul prayed for them and they were baptized in water in the name of the Lord Jesus.

And when Paul laid his hands on them, the Holy Spirit came upon them, and they spoke with tongues and prophesied.

Paul corrected their theology on the Holy Spirit and then separated the serious believers and taught them the Word of God daily in the school of Tyrannus for two years. After two years God confirmed His Word with unusual miracles. (See Mark 16:20)

Acts 19:20 says,

> "So the Word of the Lord grew mightily and prevailed."

The Word of the Lord has a life of its own and the result of it being planted in good ground was an explosion of evangelism and discipleship. From there the church grew and developed until the social impact was evident. The city's idol makers went out of business. Those who had used "curious arts" (witchcraft) came together and burned their books. And revival hit the city!

The spiritual climate, and the culture of this whole area, was changed from an idol worshipping, loveless culture to a Biblical-based Christ centered culture that had a positive impact upon that whole area of Asia.

This same sort of thing has happened in recent history. In the Welsh Revival of 1904, 150,000 people received Christ in six months out of a population of less than one million. The judges wore white gloves because there were no cases to try: no rapes, thefts, or murders.

People had become born again and were trying, with God's help, to live a life pleasing to God. It is said they had to retrain all of the donkeys that worked in the coalmines because they didn't understand the miners' commands anymore, since the miners had stopped cursing.

So they began with prayer for God to fill the spiritual hunger in the small group of believers. Next a solid core group of leaders were discipled for a two year period until the Word prevailed. When the group was ready they went public with some high profile preaching that soon caused a great stir in the city. The result was the formation of one of the great churches of the first century.

1.5 PRINCIPLES OF NEW TESTAMENT CHURCH PLANTING

The Great Commission provides us with the Biblical foundation behind our desire to plant churches. In Mark 16:15 Jesus said, "Go into all the world and preach the Gospel to every creature." There are several conclusions we can draw from this verse of Scripture.

First, the Commission is universal. The term every creature is certainly all-inclusive. There is no people group on the face of the earth that is excluded from our Commission. We cannot afford to rest until every person in our community, regardless of their race or social position, has had an opportunity to hear the Gospel presented effectively enough to allow them to make an informed decision.

Secondly, the Commission is urgent. We need to place a high priority on evangelism! Statistics show that only 15% of the churches in North America are growing. And, of those that are growing, only 1% is growing through new converts. The rest are growing through transfer growth. That tells me that we have not taken the Great Commission seriously. If we had, then all of our churches would be growing through new converts, the people we have led to the Lord. We need to discover a new urgency in our call to evangelize our communities.

And thirdly, the Commission is unfinished. The biggest mistake that most new churches make is to launch well, but then turn their attention inward and begin organizing things internally. In order to avoid losing your growth momentum – often never to be regained – you must keep the whole focus on outreach, outreach, outreach for the first 18 months or more after the Launch Day. This passage communicates personal responsibility. Jesus said, "Go ...." The Lord's Commission extends through the ages to every one of us. Jesus himself said that before his return the Gospel would be heard by the people of all nations. As Christians, we must give top priority to reaching the lost and not rest until every one has heard!

The Biblical Pattern

In the first century, churches were committed to church planting. We read of the church at Thessalonica:

> "For from you the Word of the Lord has sounded forth, not only in Macedonia and Achaia, but also in every place. Your faith toward God has gone out, so that we do not need to say anything" (1 Thessalonians 1:8).

Here we see a local church that spread the Gospel throughout their entire region. To the Thessalonians, the Great Commission consisted of more than a mandate to build their own local church. It also included the planting of new works in neighbouring communities. This group of Christians were committed to church planting and we can learn some powerful principles from what they did.

The Principle of Reproduction

From the beginning of creation we see the principle of reproduction. It is the purpose and plan of God that everything produces after its kind (Genesis 1:11). That is true of plants and animals and is also true of churches. Churches should produce after their own kind. Fruit bearing is a spiritual principle of life (John 15). Paul commissioned Timothy to commit the things he had heard to *faithful men who shall be able to teach others also* (2 Timothy 2:2). As ministers we should be reproducing ourselves in the lives of faithful men and women who will go out from us to win new souls, make new disciples and plant new churches for Christ.

This means that you can start right now with whatever model you have. Whenever we reproduce from a model that God has given us, we understand two things: that a reproduction doesn't have to be inferior to its prototype; nor does the original model have to be perfect before you start reproducing it elsewhere. For instance, take the Model-T automobile. When they first came out, they didn't even have an electric starter. You used to have to crank start them and jump out of the way before the crank broke your arm.

In fact, the electric starter was invented as a consequence of a man named Charles Kettering having his arm broken while crank starting a car.

After his arm was broken, Kettering thought, "There must be a better way to start a car than this!" So he invented the electric starter. He turned a problem into an opportunity and made a great improvement on the original invention.

The same is true with churches. We always have to start with what we have. In other words we can only do what we know how to do. But our model must be continually upgraded. We can do better and better with each successive plant. Why? For one thing, we make a lot of mistakes in the process of developing working models. New churches don't have to make the same mistakes the old ones made. They can pick up where we left off and make their things even better. We can learn from our mistakes and build upon our successes; thus enabling ourselves to build God's kingdom with a greater degree of maturity, accuracy and excellence. The more churches we plant the more efficient we should become. It is the law of production to perfection; the more you do it the better you get!

This is exactly what we've seen in Victory Churches over the last 30 years. First, God commissioned us to build a model church in Lethbridge. At the time it was one of the largest and most powerful churches in Canada. Then we built a model region of churches in Southern Alberta. After that, we went to Calgary and built a model city-wide network of churches. From there, it expanded into a model Province.

What we did in the city of Calgary we were able to reproduce in the city of Edmonton. What we produced in the province of Alberta was reproduced in provinces across Canada. And what we produced in Canada we are endeavouring to reproduce in as many nations as possible before the return of Jesus Christ. This is the principle of reproduction!

The Principle of Sending

In our desire to fulfill the Great Commission, there must always be a blending of the willingness of the individuals to initiate a new work for the Lord with the deliberate sending and commissioning of people to a work. Paul and Barnabas were sent from their home church in Antioch by the direction of the Holy Spirit (Acts 13:1-3).

Local churches must be willing to release leaders to plant new churches around the world. In the natural, a healthy body does not grow by having one cell that grows to an unlimited size. In fact, if one cell in your body grows to an unlimited size, you will end up with a malignant growth and a diseased body.

The way your body is intended to maintain its health is by division and reproduction. Cells reproduce themselves by dividing.

Some churches need to do this very thing in order to get off a plateau. Instead of becoming introverted, they need to get a Great Commission Vision. As they divide to plant a daughter church, they will experience growth themselves.

Paul and Barnabas were sent out from the church at Antioch. When people begin a new work, sometimes the Holy Spirit speaks to their hearts and they go. Other times people are sent by those in authority over them. Both methods are legitimate and scripturally based.

But remember, whenever God changes the direction of your life it should be confirmed by those in authority over you. You don't just wake up in the morning and experience a great change of direction in your life. It usually comes through seasons of prayer as God prepares your heart over a period of time.

The Principle of Giving

A giving church is a growing church. No church has ever suffered in the long run by releasing members to begin a new church. There may be a short time in which it looks like they've experienced a loss, but in the long run they will increase.

The principle of sowing and reaping works for both individuals and churches.

While it may be difficult to release some of their most productive people, mature pastors will do it because they are more interested in the total work of God than they are in their own local church. In the long run, the principle of release works in the pastor's favor. Many times the people you're not willing to release become a hindrance to you.

It's difficult to let go of people that you have invested your life into. This is especially so when they have become strong, capable, mature leaders who have made themselves almost indispensable to you. But when they are released into their next phase of ministry, it creates opportunities for many new leaders to come to the surface and not only fill the vacuum, but expand your leadership base. Like everything else, you reap what you sow. If you sow troublesome or second-rate people into church planting guess what you are going to reap? That's right – troublesome people! But when you deliberately sow your best leaders, God is faithful to bring in more tremendous people to take their place.

Ultimately, if we are willing to release people to fulfill the call of God on their lives, it will be best for the Kingdom of God and for us. What's best for the Kingdom of God is ultimately best for you and me.

When I released my first key leader to a ministry outside of my local church, I was wondering how I was going to manage without him. The Lord spoke to me through Proverbs 11:24, *"There is one who scatters, yet increases more; and there is one who withholds more than is right. But it leads to poverty."* From this passage the Lord spoke to my heart and said, "For every one you release I will give you two of like quality and character." I have been faithful to do my part, and the Lord has been faithful to do His part. I believe this is why the Lord has been able to entrust us with so many of His leaders over the years because when it's time to release we will release. We call it **Apostolic Release for World Wide Increase.**

The Principle of Faith

Over the years many pastors drift away from leadership by faith and begin to walk by sight instead. They continually watch the attendance, the church budget and the membership roll. There is nothing wrong with that as long as it doesn't become the main focus. These things are an indication of the quality of ministry that's happening in the church so we ought to pay attention to them. But we can't make ministry decisions on the basis of these things.

Establishing a daughter church demands great faith. It takes a lot of faith to release a group of people from your church to start a daughter church and then pay them for leaving on top of that! But the benefits far outweigh the problems and the cost. Don't forget that: "Without faith it is impossible to please Him" (Hebrews 11:6).

Three Kinds of Church Growth

1. The first is internal growth. This is growth in grace. Out of the good treasure of a good man's heart, he brings forth good fruit. If you want to bring forth more fruit, then increase the treasure in your heart. In our local churches we want to put value into people. We want to see them grow to the place where they are living a victorious Christian life and are reproducing themselves in others.

2. The second type is expansion growth. This is the numerical increase of the church within its own community. We all want our churches to grow. I couldn't stand just maintaining the same number of people year in and year out. God has not called us just to maintain. He has called us to "occupy until He comes" (Luke 19:10). To occupy means to take charge and manage things. And we know from the parable of the talents that the Lord expects each one of us to manage his business profitably and produce increase.

3. And thirdly there is extension growth. Extension growth takes place when a church plants a daughter church in a surrounding area, or when it releases qualified leaders to take over ministry positions in other churches. Churches located in smaller communities may never have a church with a large number of members. But, they can still be involved in this kind of church growth through the people they send out to minister in other places.

There are many different types of church plants and all kinds of ways for a new church to get up and running. No one type is superior to another but is dictated by the circumstances – the particular conditions leading to the plant and the individual strengths of the planting group. In fact the self-same local church might find itself utilizing different approaches for different plants – all at the same time.

The Mother-Daughter Model

The most basic type of plant is the mother-daughter model. This is where a group of people are released from a local church in order to form a new church somewhere within a reasonable driving distance. It's rare that people will pack up their family, change their job, and relocate to another city simply to be part of the core group of a new church. It does happen, but it would constitute the exception rather than the rule. However, many church members would be more than willing to be part of a new group within the same city. They can keep their job, house, and their kids in the same school – but instead of attending the mother church they will just drive across town to be a part of the daughter church.

It might start with a group of people who are tired of driving a long distance to their church, or perhaps a number of members have moved to a new neighbourhood. Or perhaps one of the staff is ready to step out on their own.

When two philosophies of ministry spring up within the one church, it takes great wisdom and maturity on behalf of the key leadership to be able to prevent a church split by graciously releasing one of the groups to establish a new church.

Not only are people released from the mother church, but it usually carries the majority of the financial burden for the new work as well. Their people are prepared to give above and beyond their normal donations because they feel a high level of ownership in the daughter church.

It means that for those who can't be directly involved in the new plant, they can still be a part of expanding the kingdom through their financial support. And it's not just monetary support that the mother church can provide, but often there is some under-utilized equipment lying around that finds a new life in the daughter church. In many cases the mother church is also in a position to loan trained and experienced personnel to help the younger church get established. Musicians, children's workers, a/v technicians, and others can all help to staff a beginning church until it can raise up its own workers.

The Apostolic Team Model

However, the mother-daughter model can only be effective within a small radius from the mother church. In order to plant further away, perhaps in another city or even another nation, an apostolic team is the best approach. This is where a key apostolic leader – someone with evident five-fold gifting in their life – heads up a team of other workers to form the initial core team of the new church. In most cases the leader, at least, would be supported full-time financially. The team members may or may not be supported by organizational funding, but will most likely be bi-vocational, finding employment in their new community in order to lend their skills to the establishment of the new work. A good team will look after key departmental ministries like music and children, but may include others who are just there to help wherever they're most needed. An apostolic team has a high level of dedication to the project owing to the fact that they had to re-locate their families expressly to be involved. If the team is well selected and prepared they can actually create great momentum for the launch simply by their obvious commitment.

The Single Apostolic Team Model

Like the apostolic team, a single apostle has targeted an area that is out of reach of other churches in their fellowship and can't expect much support from other local churches. His assignment is to move into the target area and pull together a team to work with before the Launch Day.

They are normally supported financially by their denomination for a certain period of time. Once a core group is formed they can begin preparations for the kick-off of the new church.

The Pioneer Church Model

A pioneer church plant begins with someone who already lives in the area. They either see a need or simply have a burden for the region and begin ministering to their neighbours on their own. In most cases the church organization first hears of them after they already have a group formed and want to take the next step up to a full-fledged church. This is what differentiates a pioneer plant from an apostolic one: an apostolic one is initiated by the organization strategically sending someone, while a pioneer plant is initiated by the planter. The level of denominational involvement here will ultimately depend on the strength of the key leader, their experience, and gifting. Are they just a gatherer who has brought a few folks together, or do they have the leadership ability to establish and grow it into a church? Any denominational support might be contingent on them being able to place a more seasoned leader in charge to launch the church and take it forward.

The Partnership Model

When a church organization takes a planting mandate seriously then they find ways to overcome the obstacles that often prevent the formation of new churches. Where there is a will to plant but no one church can provide all the necessary resources or personnel, then two or more churches can work together to give support. One may have people they can release, another may supply some equipment, but all can share in the financial burden. This approach assumes a good level of regional cooperation amongst the churches, but a well-managed plan will keep everyone informed, involved, and in prayer.

The Re-Plant Model

A re-planted church may utilize one or more of the previous models, but differs in that it starts with an existing church.

Typically this would be a church that has been in existence for several years, but has dwindled and needs a fresh start. This may be due to a history of poor management, a moral scandal with leaders, demographic changes in the neighbourhood, or any number of other factors. The church's corporate and charitable status stays intact, but the re-launch will usually necessitate a total makeover of everything else: a new vision, a new name, a new look, new leadership, and perhaps even a new location. If it is going to succeed in the community where it failed before, then the changes have to be genuine and substantial rather than merely cosmetic. But if there is no serious community stigma attached to it, the church can often get itself moving again – often with a bit of an advantage over a pioneer plant.

Adoption

When an existing church seeks affiliation with a larger group it isn't technically a church plant. But it is strikingly similar in many ways. The affiliation may involve some of the same aspects as a re-plant: a re-branding of the church which affords it a fresh promotional opportunity in the area. Coming "under new management", so to speak, puts the church in a position to invite the community at large to come and take another look at them. But before the new "grand opening day", there is a lot a preparation to do. In fact, it can take up to a year for the church to re-tool its doctrinal stance, governmental structure, and ministry priorities to bring it into line with their new affiliation.

One of the encouraging trends we are seeing as the 21st century unfolds before us is a move away from independent minded church leadership towards a more enthusiastic embrace of apostolic teamwork. The last century was marked by a philosophical approach to growing churches that viewed every local church almost as an island unto itself. It was, in part, a reaction against the rigid denominationalism of the previous century in which whole organizations of churches were directed by non-ministerial leaders who were themselves often far removed from the frontlines of local ministry. A tight grip of control over local leaders may have brought great stability, but at the expense of fresh and innovative ministries. Churches slowly became stale and stagnant, bound by religiosity, and sadly irrelevant to the communities they sought to evangelize.

As if to add fuel to this smoldering flame, along came the modern Pentecostal outpouring - the greatest move of the Spirit in recorded history. Surely history will view the 1900's as the century of the Holy Spirit! A revolt was inevitable and the 20th century saw large church movements fragmented by a desire to drink freely from this Pentecostal fountain, and shake off the heavy restraints of denominational torpor. Unfortunately, as is too often the case, the revolution drove people out of one ditch and all the way across the road into the opposite ditch. Independent churches flourished springing up everywhere almost overnight, and in too many cases, disappearing again just as rapidly as they came. Championing the idea that the local pastor was the highest authority in the church, they met for fellowship at various conventions, but rejected any form of larger organizational commitment.

But in the last few years the pendulum has swung back again, this time perhaps into a more biblical and balanced position. The doctrine of the five-fold ministry, drawn from Ephesians 4, has gained a new popularity and dedicated church leaders have sought for a road that could avoid the dangers of both denominationalism and independence while marrying the strengths of both extremes. This has led to a re-discovery of the role of apostles, prophets, evangelists, pastors and teachers – working in Spirit-led teamwork – to forge a new century of Kingdom expansion.

This isn't to imply some misguided claims of having the only living prophet, or supreme apostolic authority over others – but simply recognizing that these gifts are sown throughout the church by the Lord as the necessary tradesmen to help build his church. Apostles provide a progressive impetus, moving the church persistently toward new frontiers of growth and ministry. Prophets call us back to a deep and intimate walk with God, pointing us back to prayer and worship. Evangelists ensure that we never get caught up in doing church and forget about a world around us that is suffering and dying without hope, Pastors nurture us until we're ready to stand and fight and lead our families, churches, businesses, and cities. Teachers keep it all coherent and ordered enough to be able to reproduce again and again.

More and more churches are seeking out and embedding themselves within an apostolic network. Apostolic networks are usually smaller in size than large denominations of the past, but tied together in much tighter relationship. They are more organic than hierarchical in structure, following natural relational synapses rather than pre-determined flow-charts. And they seek to find a meaningful place of contribution from all five ascension gifts in covenantal teamwork to the ongoing growth and development of every local church.

The Victory Churches movement has been a pioneer in this regard. Embracing a five-fold theology, identifying and developing five-fold leaders, and building on a five-fold model of leadership has propelled the movement forward in rapid expansion. The benefits for newly planted churches are significant:

✓ Relational support for those on the front-lines of church planting

✓ Counsel and advice from seasoned apostles and prophets

✓ The financial resources to fully fund planting projects

✓ Ongoing prayer support from a world-wide spiritual family

Motivational Checklist:

1. Do you have a deeply rooted conviction about the importance of planting churches?

_____

_____

_____

2. Are you prepared to explain the 'why' of planting a new church? You will probably have to defend it to denominational leaders, community leaders, and people from other churches. List your reasons:

_____

_____

_____

3. What lessons in particular do some of the church plants in the New Testament teach us?

_____

_____

_____

4. Do you know which type of church plant best describes your situation? (Mother-daughter, etc..)

_____

_____

_____

SECTION 2
Preparing To Plant

2.1 ARE YOU A CHURCH PLANTER?

Although church planting bears many similarities to ordinary pastoral ministry, it also holds many unique challenges. Rather than following well-worn procedures planters have to invent their own. They have to be extraordinarily creative and able to think on their feet. They need to be able to work without many of the safety nets that other ministers often take for granted. They can't afford to be emotionally dependant on others or unable to think independently. Above all they have to be highly determined people who can encourage themselves and keep going no matter what. Are your spiritual gifts, passion, temperament, and leadership abilities ideally suited for the ministry of church planting? Here are some basic questions to start with.

1. What are your spiritual gifts?

The lone church planter should look in particular for such gifts as that of leadership, faith, evangelism, and preaching. The more gifts they have the greater will be their effectiveness. The same gifts of leadership, faith, evangelism, and preaching are necessary for a church-planting team, but may be spread out among various members of the team. The key leader should have the gift of leadership combined with evangelism and preaching.

2. What is your passion?

Passion is what you feel strongly about. It serves to both energize and provide the necessary direction for the exercise of the spiritual gifts. It is important that those on a team have the same vision, but not necessarily the same passion. Vision speaks of seeing, whereas passion speaks of feeling.

3. What is your temperament?

We are told that there are four basic personality types: choleric, sanguine, phlegmatic and melancholy. Choleric and sanguine types are extroverts. Phlegmatic and melancholy type people are more introverted. The majority of the pastoral functions involve up-front work with large numbers of people. This energizes extroverts but exhausts introverts.

Introverts function best in the team context of starting churches. Certain temperament types are preferable for those who are the primary leaders and catalysts in planting churches. However, there is a unique place for all temperaments in the context of team ministry in church planting. It is the other temperament types that fill in all the important and necessary leadership and ministry gaps.

4. What kind of leader are you?

Are you a leader or a manager, or both? If both, which is stronger? As the leadership goes, so goes the church! In terms of leadership and management, both are necessary for success. The ideal for church planting would be a combination of both roles in the person who leads the organization, a leader-manager.

5. Do you have the support of your family?

How do your spouse and family feel about being involved in a church-planting situation? Are they going to be able to provide the support and involvement you need? Are they prepared to make the necessary sacrifices?

Leaders come in all shapes and sizes, and church planters are no exception. Different personality types, different levels of maturity, and different circumstances call for different kinds of leadership. The wrong leader in the right place will struggle to produce results as much as will the right leader in the wrong place. Generally speaking there are three categories of leadership types we see in church planters:

1. Pastoral

A pastoral type of planter is one who is probably gifted as a five-fold pastor. Their primary focus is on touching people's needs, nurturing, and caring. They are most comfortable in a small group setting and usually manage to gather a core group quickly. It is often the case that they have already gathered such a group before they begin to consider transitioning it into a church plant. They tend to be highly relational individuals and will seek to grow the group chiefly through networking and personal relations. In most cases it is never their vision to plant and turn the church over to another leader, but simply to plant a church and pastor it indefinitely. Barring some exceptional circumstances, they will probably see gradual and steady growth. Transitioning to another leader may prove difficult because their leadership style is so personally tied to the congregation.

2. Catalytic

A catalytic type of leader is one who tends to provoke change and make things happen around them. They can see what needs to happen and move quickly to set things in motion. They are quick to recognize opportunities and seize them. People who want change are drawn to them because they see them as leaders who can make it happen. They tend to be better at bringing the right people together rather than training and equipping those they already have. In most cases they are not long term leaders, lacking the pastoral heart for the people and the apostolic ability to build strong foundations and build leaders who can lead.

This means that they can be instrumental in gathering an initial core group and setting things in motion, but should probably be replaced by a longer term leader soon after the launch.

3. Apostolic

Apostolic leaders make the best church planters, bringing a good balance of pastoral, catalytic, and long term leadership qualities to the table. Encompassing a great variety of personality types, apostles can be very pastorally focused as needed. They can also be engaging and evangelistic too. But their strength is in attracting and mobilizing others into leadership capacities. Their focus on structure not only helps a new church develop the necessary procedures of pastoral care and church growth, but puts things in place for the long term development of the church. Whether they remain with the new church for a few months or a few years, or leave but remain in an apostolic relationship with it - it's a good bet that they will leave it in good hands when they go.

2.3 PROFILE OF A CHURCH PLANTER

1. A planter must be spiritually strong

Church carries with it some extraordinary pressures. There is often an isolation factor, owing to the fact that it is often a pioneering endeavour. That means that the planter and his family have had to leave their familiar home church behind in order to launch the new church. And in many cases they have left friends and family behind too. Their only relational support might be their core team and they might be all newly acquainted with them! This can expose the planter and other team members to feelings of abandonment. On top of that is usually some measure of financial pressure. Every dollar counts in a planting project and there is normally a good amount of faith in the budget. These kinds of pressures can leave people very vulnerable to spiritual attack and the enemy never misses such an opportunity. All these pressures raise the stakes and keep the possibility of failure in the back of everyone's mind. It is the leader's job to keep the morale levels for his whole team high. If the planter is not spiritually strong himself, the combined weight of these factors will soon expose any weakness in his personal and family life.

Here is a checklist:

✓ Personal walk with God is strong and consistent

✓ Marriage/family is healthy and strong

✓ Positive attitude and emotional resilience

✓ Personal finances are sound

✓ Has a solid track record with home church and leaders

✓ Strong confirmation that the timing and direction is God's will

2. A planter must be an entrepreneur

Planting has many parallels to starting a new business, but with a little divine help, of course! Nevertheless it requires a keen entrepreneurial inclination. Successful entrepreneurs are visionary individuals – able to see all kinds of opportunities that others miss.

This applies to everything from finding suitable facilities to designing a creative approach to advertising, from innovative programming to finding enough chairs! Entrepreneurs are people who can see what needs to happen and can devise a way to make it happen. They may prefer to consult with a team but are perfectly capable of making and acting on their own decisions when need be. They can weigh up the risks involved and are probably more willing than most to live without normal safety nets. They are resourceful and creative when it comes to grappling with problems and see them more as simply the way forward. Entrepreneurial people are fast-thinking and flexible, quick to adapt to changing situations and ready to modify their plans accordingly.

3. A planter must be a minister

In the end, all this logistical planning and preparing is only to put you in a place to minister to people who need Jesus! Ultimately it is all about leading people to Christ, ministering to their needs, and discipling them in the Word. And in the beginning, when a new church lacks things like a nice facility, a paved parking lot, and a well-staffed nursery – the planter is the main attraction! He needs to be a good preacher, able to open the Word to people with conviction and relevance. It is his or her preaching alone that will draw people back week after week. He must be ready to counsel, pray, and minister in the gifts of the Holy Spirit at every opportunity. It is the ability to really help people grow spiritually that will win long term members.

4. The planter must be a multi-skilled individual

The more versatile a planter is the better. Pioneers must be ready for anything because anything can happen in a church plant! He should be able to assess, design, and adapt buildings for church purposes. This means a practical eye for renovation and construction realities.

Some familiarity with zoning and bylaw procedures with city councils regarding buildings and church activities will probably come in handy, too. He should be skilled at negotiating in order to secure the most advantageous deal on everything from facilities to photocopiers. Some capacity to design and approve graphic advertising layout for promotional purposes would be an asset, as well as a working knowledge of computers and other office equipment. Some acquaintance with carpentry, electrical engineering, plumbing, gas-fitting, heavy equipment operation, sky-diving, minor surgery, veterinary medicine, midwifery, and bowling may also prove helpful!

Some of the following characteristics can be learned and certainly developed, but the seed must be inherently within the church planter and his team.

An Apostle or Apostolic Person

This person is an entrepreneur. Entrepreneurs start businesses because they see a need, and find a unique way to meet the need and market the product. Church planters are the same, but instead of businesses, they start churches. A church planter should ask himself, "What can I provide that the other churches in the area aren't providing? Is there some way that I can do it different (or even better)?"

A Gatherer

A church planter gathers people like bees to honey. People are attracted to a bold, upbeat visionary. If a person cannot grow a small group; divide it into two and start a new group successfully, he is not going to be able to plant a church. A church planter must be a people person. He must take the time to develop his people skills.

Motivator / Encourager

The church planter must be one who is able to encourage himself as well as the team and the new fledgling church. A negative, melancholic person will discourage himself and others. Certainly, challenges and hard times will come as one endeavours to plant a church. But a church planter must be a David-like person, and should encourage himself in the Lord (Psalm 42:5). He cannot wait for someone else to encourage him; he must be able to encourage himself!

A Gatherer of Resources

He/she must have the skills to attract people with ability and be able to use the gifts and resources they bring into the church without being intimidated by them. Insecure people try to hinder others and keep their gifts under a bushel in order to make themselves look good. But a church planter cannot afford that luxury.

He knows that when the people under him excel, ultimately, it makes him look good!

A Relevant And Interesting Bible Teacher

Their preaching must answer the questions people are asking. It must be communicated so that both the saved and unsaved can understand it. The preaching must be meaty enough to feed the Christian who needs to be fed and challenged. Yet it needs to be simple enough for the new convert to understand and apply to his life.

The preacher is not the initial reason why people come to church the first time, but the preaching may be the reason they come back the second time. (Or don't come back!)

A Credible, Visionary Leader

People will not follow a vision, but they will follow a credible leader with a vision. Getting the people to come to your church is great, but once they have come, you must be able to keep them.

✓ Be a person of sincerity and integrity

✓ Be a lover of good and of people

✓ Be a person worthy of following

✓ Know where you're going, have a vision, set short and long term goals

✓ Be an equipper (learn to recognize potential in people, then recruit, train and delegate)

A Multi-Faceted Individual

An apostle is like the thumb on the hand being the only one that can touch every other finger.

Likewise the apostle can touch all of the other four ministry gifts mentioned in Ephesians 4:11 implying that he is a generalist. He may not be the best evangelist, pastor, prophet or teacher, but he can operate in each one of these gifts as the occasion demands. Very often he and his wife will do most of the work until people are gathered, trained and released into ministry. A flow chart is helpful at this point.

At first, the planter and his wife will be filling most of the positions. Their names will be in (almost) every box in the flow chart. Then he must pray up a storm for God to send people to take over some of the responsibilities.

A Person of Prayer

To be the leader in every area the church planter must also be first in the prayer closet! It takes time and effort to plunder hell and populate heaven! But it is time well spent. A church planter must have confidence in prayer and be prepared to engage in spiritual warfare daily! He must take every need, no matter what the size, to the Lord. This also serves as a tremendous encouragement to the whole group to be passionate in their prayers. This is the real key to success.

BE ORGANIZED!

While 'big picture' thinking is necessary, don't forget the details that will take you there. The wise church planter is organized. First he must organize himself (and his team), and then he must organize every department of the church. If the lead pastor is not a good administrator, he can call upon the gifts of the administrators in his team to help set things up so that they run smoothly. It is true that we can't build on organization, but neither can we build much without it.

God does not call a man into the ministry without calling his wife as well. The ministry call upon a woman's life is neither in opposition to nor in competition with her family. The husband and wife may differ in their gifts, talents and abilities, but they're still a team. They have to be, or there's going to be division in the home, and that's never God's will.

What causes a church planter's resignation? Many times it is caused by a lack of a spousal partnership. A church planter can't go it alone. If his spouse is not supportive and cooperative in the ministry, then their church planting assignment will be short-lived.

I say this very strongly because Amos 3:3 says, *"How can two walk together, except they be agreed?"* You can't put an ox and a racehorse together in the same yoke and expect them to be able to win the race. It's not going to happen.

It's very important that a husband and wife are going in the same direction. A church planter's wife must be in harmony with both God and her husband. She must exhibit the vision and the faith that are necessary to undertake such a task. Spousal partnership is one of the essential ingredients for a successful church plant.

If you look at the call of God on a church planter's life, you will also see a reflection of what his wife's responsibilities will be as she stands beside her husband, supporting him in all that he is doing and vice versa. This can require some adjustments within the family. It is both spouses' responsibility to pull together as a team. It is a sad thing when one is called but the other holds back because he or she has reservations or simply doesn't share their partner's vision.

When we talk about bi-vocational ministers, we are talking about those ministers who have both a secular job and are doing the work of the ministry. They have the title of pastor but receive little or no salary. Aquila, Priscilla and the apostle Paul all worked together as tentmakers while they were preaching the Gospel and planting the church in Corinth (Acts 18:1-4).

Four Criteria For Evaluating Staff Members:

1. Are they faithful and loyal?
2. Are they fruitful and effective?
3. Do they love me and my wife?
4. Do they have the vision of the house?

As a ministry develops and grows in responsibility it becomes very difficult to work both a fulltime secular job and be a fulltime minister. Bi-vocational ministers are a special group of people who, through their sacrifices, have helped to rapidly expand the kingdom of God throughout the world. They really are heroes of the faith. There are specific times when there are incredible advantages to being bi-vocational and there are times when it is more advantageous to take the plunge and believe God to supply all of your needs through your involvement in the work of the ministry.

Benefits Bi-Vocational Ministers Bring To The Table

1. They are not a financial drain on the church; in fact they earn a salary and tithe on it. This makes them a financial contributor to the church.

2. They are mixing with people in the community on a regular basis, which gives them opportunity to make inroads into the hearts of the lost and backslidden. This is especially valuable for those planting a new church. They have contacts and information about the community that would otherwise be unavailable to them.

3. It gives the new minister time to grow and mature in ministry and possibly create a paid position for themselves. There is far less pressure on everybody in this kind of situation.

4. It gives the senior leader or overseer the extra help they need. It also gives them an opportunity to prove the call and develop the gifting in an up-coming leader.

5. Some people have a number of different streams of income-investments, rental properties, real estate, or their own business. Others are professionals who love both their profession and the ministry and can handle both. They would rather volunteer their time or just take a small salary to allow others to be put on paid staff.

6. Younger people need to be stretched and older ones need to learn to delegate, motivate and mobilize those with the desire to grow in the ministry.

7. Young potential ministers need to be stretched to increase their capacity so that they do not crack under pressure at a later date in their ministry. Bi-vocational ministry provides this opportunity without many of the risks that failure can bring.

8. Good volunteers do not always make good staff members. If you are not careful you may feel obligated and end up putting the wrong person on staff. When they are volunteers, everything they do is appreciated, but when they are paid staff members, what you appreciated before is now expected. However, some are best left to operate as volunteers.

9. Bi-vocational workers have plenty of opportunity to try their hand at a wide variety of tasks related to the work of the ministry. This helps them to find out where their passion is and what brings forth the most fruit in their ministry. Passion and ability help to reveal destiny.

2.7 ACCURACY: GOING TO THE RIGHT PLACE

It happened after this that David inquired of the Lord, saying, "Shall I go up to any of the cities of Judah?" And the Lord said to him, "Go up." David said, "Where shall I go up?" And He said, "To Hebron." (2 Samuel 2:1)

The right person, going to the right part of the right city at the right time is vital. God will not bless you doing anything just anywhere. He will bless you when you are where you are supposed to be, doing what you are supposed to be doing with what He gave you. Sometimes it can take years to recover from inaccuracy.

STRATEGIES USED BY VICTORY CHURCHES FOR DISCOVERING, DEVELOPING AND DEPLOYING PEOPLE INTO VOLUNTEER, PART-TIME AND FULL-TIME SERVICE

✓ The Timothy apprenticeship type program of theory and practical on-the-job experience.

✓ Leading Edge—extra leadership type training for those already involved in ministry.

✓ Victory Bible College—full-time/part-time in-house or online courses

✓ Finishing Edge—a week-long course designed not necessarily to train leaders, but to find out how developed they are, and what kind of ministry position they are best suited for.

✓ Partial sponsorships through VCI for new staff members in new positions. This calls for sacrifice on behalf of the individual; the local church and the national movement. This puts people on a fast track into full-time Christian service.

✓ Emerging Leaders Program – identifies and trains upcoming leaders within their own local church through a directed program of studies and mentoring.

✓ Small group ministry within the local church. This gives potential ministers an opportunity to prove and develop their call while still working in a full-time secular position. We call this the Exodus 18 principle from the advice that Jethro gave to Moses to set in leaders of tens, fifties, hundreds and thousands. No one starts out as a leader of thousands, but the Exodus 18 principle provides a safe environment for the preparation, proving and promotion of new leaders.

✓ Church Planting Schools where we mentor leaders and train students in the dynamics of planting New Testament Churches.

✓ World missions training seminars for all who will be going on the mission field with Victory Churches.

Provision and power follow God's purpose. Jesus sent the 70 disciples out two by two. He told them not to take a purse with them and said, *"Whatever city you enter and they receive you, eat such things as are set before you" (Luke 10:8).* He told them to keep moving until they were received and when they were received, to stay there and minister to the people and they will give you food and shelter. In other words, find God's purpose and you will find God's provision.

Once they had learned this lesson He let them take a purse.

Without provisions there was a sense of urgency about finding the right location. He told them to keep moving until they did. Had they taken a purse with a lot of money, it would have enabled them to stay too long in the wrong place. Some church planters, even experienced ones, might be given quite a lot of money for a church plant and then spend most of their money in the wrong location. They liked the area, bought a house there and worked very hard doing all of the right things, but they were in the wrong location. God's will always has to do with people and places.

God plants us in a definite place at a definite time to accomplish a definite purpose. It pays to take the time and be diligent to find that place. There is no place that is out of place when you're in God's place!

Many of the principles we're going to discuss in this chapter are very simple, but it's for that very reason that so many people overlook them. It is the little foxes that spoil the vine.

Sometimes it is just a little adjustment that will cause us to succeed in an area in which we've struggled in the past.

Spy Out The Land

The first thing you need to do when you're considering an area for a church plant is to drive around the area and pray. You want to be led by the Holy Spirit. As you drive through the area, observe the people. Look for potential church facilities. Look for schools, community halls, churches, theatres and lease rentals. Don't eliminate anything simply because you don't want to go there. Keep your heart open and surrender your will to the will of God. Jesus said, "*Ask, and it will be given to you; seek, and you will find; knock, and it will be opened to you*" (Luke 7:7). If you do these things you will find the right location and the right facility and you and your team will know it.

In Numbers 13, the Israelites went into the land of Canaan to spy out the land. They took a leader from each of the tribes and entered the land. In modern-day terms, you would take the leaders of each of the different areas of ministry that you're going to have in your church.

Take the people who will look after the youth and children's ministries. Drive around and pray in the Spirit. What is the Holy Spirit saying to each of you? If you know for sure this is the city you are being called to, then it's just a matter of finding out where in the city He wants you to plant (or, in the case of a replant, where he wants you to relocate).

Attend every fruitful church in the area to see what is working and what isn't. Can you do it any different or better? If there are several churches that are the same flavour as your church will be, you may want to reconsider your plans to plant there.

It's wise to determine the approximate age of the area you are considering. If you go into an older area, chances are that you will find a lot of older people who are set in their ways. It may be better to go into a new development. Most of the residents will be young families with no definite mindset towards religion and no real commitment to any church.

What is the population of the area? What is the growth potential for a new church? Is it transient? (Every city has certain areas that are transient.) How do you know? There will be a lot of rental apartments and starter homes. People go there to buy a more inexpensive home just to build up some equity. As soon as that happens, they will sell that home and move to another area of the city. In that kind of a location, you will have a large turnover of people in your church. God still may want you to be there, but you need to know in advance the environment in which you are about to plant.

Is there an expected increase of population in the area you're planning to go? Look at the city's plans for growth. Which way is the city moving? Where are the new homes being built? That's the place to go, because you have potential new church members moving into the area all the time - people who want to put down roots, make new friends and become part of their new community. A new church in that kind of an area has that a wonderful opportunity to bring the community together around the life changing Word of God.

Are there pockets of ethnic groups in the area? Did you know that there are mission fields in every one of our towns and cities? There are pockets of ethnic groups that have never been reached with the Gospel. If you're going to plant in that area, you need to learn about the culture of those ethnic groups, so that when you go to reach out to them you already know something about what they believe. Then you will be more prepared to answer their questions and win them to Jesus.

Culture

Culture here refers to the lifestyle and the mindset of those who live around your church. How do they think? What is their spiritual background?

For instance, if you're located in a predominantly Catholic area, then you should be aware of that. If you were to get up on Sunday morning and preach against Mary and the rosary, it certainly wouldn't help you influence people and win them to Jesus. You have to be "wise as serpents, and harmless as doves" (Matthew 10:16).

But of course you shouldn't be preaching against Mary anyway. Get up there and preach Jesus!

Stay away from those things that you know are going to affect the way people receive you and your message.

What are the interests of the people in your area? Are they interested in art and music? If they are, then you can major on the arts in your church. Where do the people hurt? Are they poor? Are there a high percentage of divorces? What are they afraid of?

Some people are very private. A telephone campaign won't work in some areas. People won't respond to telephone or door to door solicitation. In other areas, they are totally open to a telephone campaign. Find out what they're afraid of. Some people don't want you in their homes. They don't want you too close to them. You have to know these things. The more you know about the people in the area you're concentrating on, the easier it will be to reach them.

One of the major barriers to church growth is people-blindness. In other words - being blind to the people you're trying to reach, being unaware of social and cultural differences between them. The best way to find out the culture, mindset and lifestyle of people is to talk to them.

Determine the spiritual climate over the area. Usually there are strong demonic forces and strongholds that must be broken over a region before you can successfully minister to the people there. You may have to go in months in advance and do spiritual warfare before you can actually plant a church.

Talk to other pastors who have been there for a long period of time. What do they know about the people in that area? What are the un-churched like in the area? For example, un-churched intellectuals are very different from un-churched farmers, or un-churched immigrants. Each of these groups has a different mindset, different backgrounds, focus and interests.

Going To The Right People Group

To be effective in planting and building a great church means first identifying the people you want to reach. Each individual in the Body of Christ has to know what God has called him or her to. Paul was called to the Gentiles, while Peter was the apostle to the Jews.

If you're called to a downtown street ministry, then go and minister to those people according to the ability that God has given you. If you love those people, but aren't called to minister to them, then let someone else minister to them and then support those outreaches the best way you can. Discover, define, develop and deploy your own gifts to do what God has called you to do. Your passion and ability help reveal your destiny.

When God gives you an assignment, He also gives you the passion and ability to fulfill it. Before we move into a particular part of a city, it is important from a practical standpoint to do the demographics.

2.8 RESEARCHING DEMOGRAPHICS

Once you have determined which city or community you plan to target you need to learn everything that you can about the community. What kind of a church you plant/build will to a large extent be determined by who you are trying to reach. A traditionally styled church complete with hymnbooks and pews may be perfectly healthy but unable to grow because it is situated in a neighbourhood that is primarily populated with Baby-Boomers. Perhaps a declining economy is taking people out of the community and out of the church regardless of its health. Or maybe a booming economy is bringing many new people into the church and masking underlying problems that, if not addressed, could seriously damage its work in the future. The world around us is continually evolving new fashions, trends of thought, and values. A church that was on the cutting edge only ten years ago will be seriously out of date if it hasn't changed anything in those same ten years. It's a different world today. And today, more than ever, church leaders must be culture-conscious if they wish their ministry to remain fruitful. You should know more about your target community than anyone!

Information about the target community can be gleaned from:

✓ Census data and demographic surveys available from the City Hall

✓ Researching community history at the local library

✓ First hand observations from walking and talking in the neighbourhood

Here are some research questions that you need to find the best answers to that you can:

1. How many people live within a 30-minute drive?

What is the population of your drawing area? The size of a community will dictate the number of people you can reasonably expect to attend your church.

2. Is the prevalent mindset urban or rural?

People's mentality and lifestyle changes as you move from urban to rural. In the countryside people are much more sensitive to community opinion and much slower to takes risks that will upset neighbourly relations. They cling to well-worn traditions more tightly. They may be slower to make spiritual decisions, but they tend to stick to them once committed. City people tend to be bolder in their lifestyle choices, including church. They care less what people think because there is a higher level of anonymity.

3. What are the primary types of employment?

Is this a farming or fishing based economy? Oil business? Banking and white-collar work? Mining? Manufacturing? The predominant occupation will attract a certain kind of people to an area and a wise church gears its ministry to meet the needs of those people.

4. Is the local economy progressing or regressing?

A church could be doing all the right things but if the big mine has closed and the streets are littered with For Sale signs then a lack of church growth doesn't necessarily point to problems within the church at all. Boomtowns tend to attract people who are willing to take a chance and try something new. Aggressive churches usually prosper in these types of communities.

5. What is the economic bracket of the target community?

No church is called to reach everyone. How much money people have dictates many of their lifestyle choices, social conventions, and the type of church they prefer. A church that tries to reach everyone will probably fail to reach many. When formulating the church's mission statement they need to ask themselves who they are really called to reach. Look around at the existing congregational members and ask, "What income bracket are we?" This will help the church to develop outreaches and ministries that touch actual needs around them.

6. What does a demographic survey of the area reveal?

How many homeless live in your neighbourhood? How many single parent families? What percentage are on social assistance? How many students? A demographic survey is an in depth analysis of the make-up of the city/community. These are regularly undertaken by different levels of government and are usually available from city hall. A demographic survey will record people's age, gender, marital status, occupation, education level, racial background, number of children and so on. For a church wondering why their beautiful little stone chapel, solid oak pews and fine organ music isn't attracting people – the answer might lie in that they are located in a neighbourhood that is populated with Baby-Boomers.

They want rock & roll, active children's ministries and sports in their church! Maybe the pastor's lofty messages aren't connecting because 75% of the community are high school dropouts!

7. What percentage of the community are first generation immigrants?

The world is increasingly becoming a global village. Although some communities in North America wouldn't know an immigrant if they ran over one with their truck, in many cities the count can be as high as 80% of the community. This drastically alters the way a church will seek to minister there. ESL classes, services in another language or with an interpreter may be necessary to evangelize the area. Church leaders may need to become very familiar with immigration law in order to help new people to find a home in North America and find Christ as their Saviour.

8. What religious factors influenced the history of the community?

Many cities have a religious history. Perhaps the initial settlement was a monastery or a convent. Perhaps a Methodist revival swept the community in its infancy and set the spiritual tone for years to come. When people immigrated to North America they brought their religious convictions with them and their influence can be traced all the way down to the present. Studying the history of your community can expose many deeply buried convictions that still influence individuals and families today.

9. What other churches are within a 30 thirty minute drive?

How big are they? How healthy are they? Drawing a "spiritual map" can be an eye opening exercise!

Assign a different colour to every kind of denomination and church in your area. Take a map of your area and stick a dot of that colour where it belongs on the map. You might be surprised what you learn. There is somewhat of a "competition factor" in church building that it is wise to take into account when deciding where to locate a church. Too many similar churches farming the same area are wasting their resources. However, just because a church building is located there doesn't necessarily mean that there is a conflict. You need to assess the impact of that church. Some have become irreversibly insular over time and cannot effectively impact their community any longer. God does not work through one local church to reach a city. Whatever their name, they reflect the wonderful diversity of the Body of Christ and it takes the whole church to reach the whole city.

10. How is the relationship between the churches in the area?

Is there a functioning ministerial association? How well do churches in the city get along? Division and hostility between churches undermines the work and the credibility of all churches. Refusing to forgive and heal old rivalries can open a door for the enemy in a community. Always seek to be an agent of reconciliation. How is your church's relationship with others? It is important to establish and maintain an attitude of respect and support for every other pastor and church. Joint services, regular prayer meetings with other pastors, and bigger city-wide projects provide opportunities to foster and protect these relationships.

11. What attitudes does the community hold toward church in general?

Are you guessing or do you have first-hand knowledge? Rick Warren launched the now famous Saddleback Church by personally doing door-to-door surveys of his neighbourhood to see for himself what people were doing, thinking, and expecting in a church.

12. Can you name the top three needs in your target community?

This kind of information can be gathered from a number of sources: recent demographic surveys, first-hand interaction with community members, feedback from church members, input from police and social workers.

13. How would you view the neighbourhood if you were a policeman?

It is an eye opening experience for most pastors to spend the night driving the beat with a local policeman. Cities in particular, have a whole other culture that only comes out at night! Do you know the crime statistics in your area? Knowing the crime rate as compared to other similar communities helps you see the community from another side.

Your ultimate goal, through all the programs and activities of your church, is to change that crime rate for the better!

14. Who is your competition?

This doesn't refer to other churches. You might be surprised to learn that the real enemy of church growth isn't the devil, but the local minor hockey league! What is your community so busy doing that they don't have time to come to church? Shift work keeps many families reeling and unable to attend regular services. Scheduling a worship service for a Friday or Saturday night can suddenly reach a whole new constituency. Creative small groups can find a niche almost anywhere, meeting in restaurants, hockey arenas, exercise clubs, and so on. The second way churches can fight the competition is to target strategic initiatives into the communities that will help change and eliminate current obstacles. Form a protest that puts a halt to shift work. Lobby to have one night a week "hockey or ball game free". The possibilities are as numerous as the problems themselves.

15. What major institutions dominate the community?

If so, how do they affect people's attitudes and behaviours? Do you live in a college town? A company town? Do a majority of people all work for the same company?

In such situations there are usually two kinds of people – those who work for the company, and those who used to work for the company and are bitter and hostile. Which camp would you prefer to build your church upon if you want it to grow and succeed? Huge institutions definitely affect the community and therefore how the church ministers to the community.

16. What is the prevailing political preference?

A church disappointed over the lack of interest in their family seminars might find the answer in discovering that the people in their electoral zone consistently vote pro-abortion or pro-homosexual! Political preferences are usually an outgrowth of people's values. Following the political issues of your area can help you position the church to be more effective.

17. How is the church's relationship with city hall?

Churches have to deal with city hall when it comes to zoning approval for building, building permits, community facility rentals, sign placement, noise bylaws, and a host of other issues. It is worth your while to cultivate goodwill with those who can potentially raise much opposition to the church's work if they so wish. Hint: politicians like to see churches that do visible, measurable good works – feeding the hungry, housing the homeless, beautifying neighbourhoods, etc..

18. Is sub-culturization a factor?

Every community is a collection of subcultures. Some are racial, some are economic, some are lifestyle oriented, and some are career or recreation based. New churches can have a quick start by tapping into a subculture. But if the particular group is fairly insulated from the community, for example a small community of Croatian speaking refugees, the church may find itself unable to reach out beyond their initial success. In order to grow, the church must present a vision of the Gospel that shines as a greater commonality than any other differences people may have.

2.9 THE LEGAL ASPECTS OF A NEW CHURCH

In Canada and the USA a church is both a non-profit corporation and a federally registered charitable organization. Most churches incorporate so that the church becomes a legal entity which can handle finances and own property. One of the principal advantages of incorporating is that it limits the legal and financial liability of the directors of the incorporation. Normally state or provincial incorporation is sufficient because the average church doesn't do business on a national level. This process can take up to six months and therefore should be initiated as soon as the decision is made to plant. Getting some legal help may speed the process along. Typically you must have a minimum of three "arms-length" individuals to serve as directors, a statement of purpose, and a set of by-laws to incorporate.

Local church bylaws and related documents are usually provided by the denomination. Start with them and adapt to suit local government policy as needed. If there is no one locally that can be a director, we often use other Victory pastors in the region who could serve in that capacity. This is an excellent way to put the church into proper legal form without running the risks involved in placing unproven leaders in a place of authority. They might hold these positions for one or two years before being replaced with local leaders. In the government's eyes, directors are legally responsible for the affairs of the church and are required to exercise "due-diligence" in knowing what is going on. The church must file an Annual Corporate Return to the Corporations Branch.

Secondly, the church must be registered with the federal revenue agency in order to issue official receipts for charitable donations. Donation receipts must carry the church's charitable number and be issued by the end of February each year. An annual return must also be filed with the federal revenue service.

The church should also carry adequate property and liability insurance. Even though the premiums are an extra expense at a time when income is low, people today are not afraid to launch lawsuits against churches. Many brokers offer special policies and rates for churches and ministers. It pays to shop around.

2.10 THE FINANCIAL SIDE OF CHURCH PLANTING

Proper management of finances is essential to insure both the viability and the credibility of the new church. One of people's top criticisms of the church is that "it's all about money". All it takes to reinforce their negative suspicions is the tiniest hint of monetary mismanagement, whether caused by fraudulent intentions or by carelessness. A wise planter will go overboard to make the handling of the church's funds as transparent and accountable as possible. The planter should never mix church and personal finances. The church should be a separate legal entity with its own bank account, chequebook, and accounting books. Open a bank account for the church with yourself and at least one other "arms-length" person as signing authorities. This allows you to create a paper-trail for every transaction. Avoid paying for things with cash for this very reason – there is no paper-trail.

When people do examine the financial statements and they see that there were large cash withdrawals it raises eyebrows, even though there is an explanation offered. Stick to writing cheques and keeping receipts and everyone can see exactly how funds have been handled. All incoming funds should be deposited to the church and all expenses, including salaries and reimbursements for out-of-pocket expenses should be paid from the church account by cheque. Keep accurate financial records of every transaction including receipts, cancelled cheques, and so on. If this isn't your forte, find a bookkeeper who can keep it all in order with a brief once-a-week visit for a minimal cost.

There are numerous laws affecting the way charities handle their finances. You or your accountant must be familiar with all IRS/Revenue Canada requirements and make sure that the church is in compliance. Make yourself accountable to your core group through a regular monthly financial report. When I've done this in the early stages of a church plant I've had people tell me, "We don't want to hear all that. We trust you. Just go ahead and do what you need to do." But I insisted they go through it with me anyway. The result is that in over 20 years of church planting I have not had one instance of financial scandal or accusation arise!

Budget for regular items such as salaries, facilities costs and advertising, and review your budget regularly. Calculate and submit organizational tithes and missions funds (or denominational dues) from the very beginning. Although it is tempting to reason that all possible funds are needed for the plant and that the church can begin to tithe once it is better established, the truth is that there will never be a better time. Teach your people about the importance of a biblical perspective on handling finances. Insist on the importance of tithing and offerings and demonstrate generosity both as a leader and as a church. God will honour and bless your faithfulness in this with sufficient funds to meet every need.

2.11 FUNDING A CHURCH PLANT

Funding is a critical issue. Eventually the team will have to acquire some initial financing, one way or another for things like:

✓ Advertising exposure and materials (banners, signs, brochures, etc)

✓ Web/online costs

✓ Audio/visual equipment

✓ Salaries

✓ Children's ministry supplies

✓ Facility costs

✓ Office supplies

✓ Coffee!

Typically launch funds will be provided by either the mother church or the covering denomination or both. But often they are only able to supply the bare minimum. If the planting team wishes to do anything on a grander scale they may have to consider additional means of raising funds. These could include contributions from the core team itself. No one is more committed to the new church than these key players and some may be in a position to make significant personal donations, arrange loans, or solicit corporate donations from businesses they are connected with. Perhaps their own family would help sponsor them on a church planting venture, especially if it involves them relocating to another city, state, or province. Even corporate sponsorships could be solicited if the business is ethically compatible with the church and if the church's advertising campaign can offer sufficient exposure for them. For example, we have had Christian real estate agents who would sponsor the cost of a flyer campaign in return for featuring their name and logo somewhere on the page. You could do the same thing with all kinds of different businesses – cafes, taxi companies, grocery stores, and so on. The opportunities are unlimited!

Of course the other side of raising income is lowering expenses. A good church planter tends to be an entrepreneurial thinker – resourceful, creative, and a skilled negotiator. There are often many ways to acquire what you need short of just paying full retail for it. Certain types of equipment are generic to church work – sound systems, Sunday school furniture and curriculum, chairs, and so on. In many cases there is a church somewhere with just the equipment you need stashed away in a back room taking up valuable storage space. They might be more than happy to donate it to a new church plant. As a church we are in the fortunate position of being able to offer a tax deductible receipt for the donation of goods and services as well as monetary gifts. You need to be careful that government guidelines for this are followed closely, but for the donor the pay-off is in lowering their own taxable income and keeping that tax money in their own pocket at tax time. This could work with everything from church furniture to real estate. For example, suppose the landlord is asking $2000/month rent for a facility. In many cases we have successfully negotiated a lease to pay only $1000/month and a tax receipt for $1000/month.

And when it comes to real estate, few things have as many different ways to approach financing. You could make an offer to purchase with a portion of the price being paid with a tax receipt. You might negotiate a deal to start at a lower rent than the owner is asking but increase it gradually as the church grows to finally pay what they want or even a little more.

Many churches have worked a rent-to-purchase agreement where they rent the building for a certain time with the understanding that a portion of the rent will become their down payment to purchase. Even that financing could be a conventional loan through a bank or perhaps the owner will be willing to carry the mortgage.

Bartering for services is also a way to get what you need without cash. For example, perhaps someone or a company would be willing to loan the use of their truck for a day in return for the youth group washing and polishing it! A shrewd money manager always looks for ways to double up on expenditures – hanging curtains around the walls of a dingy room can save you the cost of paint, add decorative warmth to the room, and help with the acoustics – all with one expenditure.

Buying bulk or in larger quantities can really lower your cost per item. Even in purchasing things like sound systems. Instead of buying one system you may be able to get a significant discount by purchasing two or three entire systems, and then re-sell the others at their retail value and apply the profit to lower the cost of your own system. If the budget is so tight that you can't advertise through newspapers and similar media, sometimes an event like a bake sale or a theatrical performance can reach just as many people just as effectively and have them pay you for the privilege! The possibilities are endless!

All of these things assume that someone on the team has some good negotiating skills or that they are willing to develop them. It should be said though, that no matter how hard you negotiate for things, you should never present yourself (and by association your church and the whole kingdom of God) as being poor and destitute, or cheap and stingy. Negotiating for a better price on things is respected and in many cases, expected. But that is a very different thing than whining, snivelling, begging, or cheating. You need to see everything you do is part of your evangelism program!

Dealing with landlords and businessmen is also a tremendous opportunity to involve them in the church, minister to them and their families, and lead them to the Lord. Many people will be more impressed by how the church does its business than they ever will by its formal outreach efforts. The guiding principle in negotiating is to find out what the other party really needs and then find a way to supply their need without dipping into your limited reserves of cash. You would think, for example, that all a landlord wants is the rent money. But in fact the whole management of the property might be a tremendous headache for them. They might be more than willing to give the church a huge discount in the rent in return for you taking over some aspects of the property management for them. Maybe they are holding fast to a high figure for the rent. But maybe it's because they need the money to cover medical expenses for a family member. Praying for their healing might just result in a miracle, a very happy landlord, and a miraculously low rent for the church! Find out what people really need and look for a way you can meet that need besides paying cash.

And as for purchasing priorities, don't buy anything pre-launch that you can live without till post-launch. You may dream of a gold-plated pulpit to preach from, but it won't help you launch the church. Let the members give it to you for a 25th church anniversary present instead! The vision that you hold of what the church will be as a finished product won't be built in a day. Some things may come into place quickly, but others you will need to work towards for years to come. Use your pre-launch funds to launch as big and as well as possible. Once the church is going and growing, the incoming funds will also increase and allow you to do more.

Along that same line, try not to purchase anything that will be useful exclusively in the launching phase. Always try to "kill two birds with one stone." In other words, invest in things that can be used both for the launching of the church and for its ongoing ministry. If you buy a bunch of lumber and build a big sign to promote your opening day, plan to reuse the lumber (after the 30 day municipal sign permit expires!) to build the platform for the children's church room. Try to always evaluate every purchase with an eye to its utility in both the immediate and long term plan.

2.11 PREPARATORY CHECKLIST

1. Are you called to plant? List three reasons why you believe you are:

a _____

_____

_____

b _____

_____

_____

c _____

_____

_____

2. Would you call yourself an entrepreneur? What endeavours have you pioneered that demonstrated those abilities?

_____

_____

_____

3. What vocational skills do you have and how would you utilize them to finance yourself if required?

_____

_____

_____

4. Name three resources that you have researched to learn more about your target community:

a _____

_____

_____

b _____

_____

_____

c _____

_____

_____

5. Have you ever completed the necessary forms for incorporation and charitable registration? Who will you use as incorporating directors to file the application?

a _____

_____

_____

b _____

_____

_____

c _____

_____

_____

SECTION 3
The Planting Process

3.1 THE IMPORTANCE OF CLEAR VISION

Vision springs from our purpose. Your goals spring from your vision, and your plans spring from your goals. If you have the wrong purpose, you will have the wrong vision. If you have the wrong vision, you will set the wrong goals. If you set the wrong goals, you will make the wrong plans, and as you may have discovered there is no favor outside of the will of God. "And we know that all things work together for good to those who love God, to those who are the called according to His purpose" (Romans 8:28).

Our Victory Statement of Purpose, for example, is:

a) local,

b) regional,

c) national, and

d) international.

It is a global, worldwide, unlimited vision, that builds unlimited churches, creates unlimited opportunities that help to grow unlimited Christians and release unlimited power.

THE BASIC PURPOSE OF OUR LOCAL CHURCHES IS THREE-FOLD:

- ✓ To reach every available person at every available time by every available means with the Gospel of Jesus Christ.
- ✓ To establish them in the local church, teaching and training them to become like Christ.
- ✓ To mobilize the army of God, to help each person to find his or her place and function in the body of Christ

THE BASIC PURPOSE OF A NATIONAL CHURCH PLANTING ORGANIZATION IS THREE-FOLD:

- ✓ To train up and release five-fold ministry giftings into Holy Spirit directed service.
- ✓ To plant church-planting churches that will continue to work together for the purpose of reproducing leaders and churches.
- ✓ To give apostolic oversight and direction to churches planted, assuring healthy growth.

THE BASIC PURPOSE OF VICTORY CHURCHES INTERNATIONAL IS FOUR-FOLD.

- ✓ To plant church-planting organizations in as many nations of the world as is possible before the return of Christ.
- ✓ To raise up apostolic teams with a key leader in each nation.
- ✓ To release developed five-fold ministry giftings into Holy Spirit directed service to the nations.
- ✓ To work together as nations united with a common purpose to reach the world with the Gospel of Jesus Christ.

We start in our Jerusalem and then expand to our Judea, our Samaria, and on to the uttermost regions of the earth. We seek to think globally and then act locally.

The way you think will determine how you act. If you think locally, then you will act in a very limited way. When you think globally, it will change the way you act locally. God's power is released to fulfill God's purpose; not to make us feel good, not to give us goose bumps, but to fulfill His purpose and expand His kingdom.

The statement of purpose tells us why an organization exists. Leaders look firstly for the purpose of an organization and find out who the leader is later. Followers firstly find out who the leader is and discover the purpose later. Leaders ask themselves, "Why does this organization exist and is it doing what it's supposed to be doing?" The purpose of any local church is primarily dictated by the Great Commission and varies little from church to church or from age to age: evangelism, discipleship, and the development of new leaders.

Vision flows from purpose and addresses the question of 'what?' What must we do to fulfill our purpose? What will it look like when we get there? Strategy asks 'how' we will proceed.

It's about plans, structures, and tactics. And goals give us the 'when' - setting up some milestones that show us whether or not we are making any progress.

No matter which approach you use to launch, you will need to have a clear and compelling grasp of the purpose and the vision of the church. The planting team needs to take time to define their vision for the church in great detail. The clearer the picture of the finished product you can show people, the easier it will be to enlist them in the cause. Creating a vision statement will help ensure that the many other aspects of the planting strategy are consistent, including:

✓ Where to plant

✓ What type of campaign strategy to utilize

✓ Style of advertising and promotional materials

✓ Style of services

✓ Selection of suitable team members

✓ Types of ministries to create

A vision statement should reflect a number of factors, including the priorities and overall objectives of the organization or denomination that the church is a part of. Secondly, a statement of vision needs to reflect the needs and the opportunities of their target community.

Since the vision statement will be the basis of planning ministries and outreaches and give direction to the overall public profile of the church, it needs to be thoughtfully tied to the specific needs and opportunities of its target community. A third consideration is the particular values and priorities of the planting team. A clever slogan may touch all the right bases for the church, but if it doesn't awaken the passion of the leaders, then it isn't going to transfer any passion to the congregation either. In other words, it's not enough to just have a good vision; it has to be our vision! And lastly, a good vision statement should take into consideration the long term objectives of the church. Changing vision statements and advertising tag lines too radically and too often can give the church a public perception of being uncertain of where it fits or what its purpose is at all. The right approach is to prayerfully settle on a long term mission and let the promotional version evolve slowly over the years.

Creating Ownership

One of the greatest results of a well-crafted vision is that it gives everyone, especially the core group, a "buy-in" opportunity. Having enthusiastic ownership of the vision is a critical ingredient in successfully launching and growing a new church. Making the vision "plain" really allows people to "run" with it. (Hab 2:2) Initially the leader may have to provide most of the vision. In fact it should be said, if he can't sell a compelling vision of the new church to his own core team, he will almost certainly not be able to sell it to anyone else! He needs to be able to paint a vivid enough picture of the future of the new church that others can see it too. And when others see what you see, they tend to feel what you feel, give like you give, work like you work, and generally do what you would do! On top of that, shared ownership in the vision is like glue that binds the team together with one heart and one mind. Maintaining team unity is always essential in church planting. It is, after all, front line spiritual warfare! A divided team is a defeated team. The stronger the commitment of each member to the dream they share, the more naturally that unity occurs.

The following is a process that can help guide you and your team as you seek to capture the heartbeat of God for your church and put it into a powerful, motivational vision statement that can draw people to the church and propel the church forward in its mission. It starts with defining what your top values or priorities will be. This is what gives a church a unique personality. There are hundreds of things that a church could do – all good and all necessary. But no local church can do them all. Clarifying values means choosing which, of all the good things you could do, will be your top priorities. Once those are selected you can pull out your thesaurus and craft a one sentence summation of each of them. This will serve to both shape the next step of designing your vision statement, and provide a great tool for teaching new members about your vision and values as a church. Once these are in place you can draw on them to begin putting your vision statement together.

These are deep, searching questions to answer and shouldn't be just quickly thrown together.

Take the time to work through them prayerfully and thoughtfully. They are just some tools to help you focus your mind on grasping as strongly as possible, what is God's plan and purpose for your new work. This is not something that you want to get wrong, or just end up with a superficial grasp of. Work it out!

3.2 DETERMINING CORE VALUES

If you're starting from scratch to develop your church's vision statement it will help to first define your core values. Core values are those passionately held beliefs that determine everything else we do. They help define who we are, both to ourselves and others. They are not to be confused with a doctrinal statement, but rather try to define the particular personality of the church. They could include everything from a strong emphasis on ministering to children to a passion for political activism. From integrity to non-judgmentalism. From cultural relevance to doctrinal accuracy, anointed worship, helping the poor, world missions, or conserving traditions. Clarifying what's most important to the church puts you in a great position to start defining your vision.

1. Sit down with your core group and list as many values you can think of that characterize your ideal vision of the church. It doesn't matter how many you end up with at this point, just write them all down.

2. Then go through the list you've made and rate each one from 1 (lowest value) to 5 (highest value).

3. Go back over the list and highlight those that rated a 4 or a 5. Discard the rest or blend them into one of the top rated ones.

4. Now narrow this list down to between 5–10 values in order of priority. All churches share much the same overall values, but your uniqueness lies in how you prioritize them.

5. Lastly, start to refine and detail your concepts into one sentence statements.

Here are some examples:

"Christ-Centred – we believe the Christian life begins with saving faith in Jesus, is directed by our love for Jesus, and ends in eternity with Jesus. We want everything we do as a church to reflect the person, the purpose, and the power of Jesus Christ."

"Bible-Based Teaching – we hold the Word of God to be true and every contrary circumstance subject to change."

"Spiritual Empowerment – we are fervently committed to experiencing the continual empowerment and leading of the Holy Spirit in our lives and our church."

"Faith in Action – we believe the Great Commission should be carried out by all believers using their unique personality, gifts, and experiences. We share the Gospel through our lifestyle, our words, and the demonstration of the power of God."

Review and re-edit each statement until you are satisfied that it truly reflects your deepest values and expresses God's purpose for your church. Then write them down in the space below.

These are your core values:

1 _____

2 _____

3 _____

4 _____

5 _____

6 _____

7 _____

8 _____

9 _____

10 _____

Now we can get to work drafting a vision statement. A vision statement is a powerful, concise description of what your church is all about - a detailed picture of the finished product. It should capture the purpose, style, and impact of your ministry in a brief but memorable statement of one or two sentences.

Don't try to include all your values, rather craft a statement that seems to blend them all together into one powerful statement that every one of your values could say, "Amen" to. Experiment with different adjectives and phrasing. Go for words that are clear and forceful rather than clever and catchy. A well-crafted vision statement can be used in many situations, either written or verbal, to explain your vision and enlist the support of others.

Spend all the time you need re-working it. In one concise and memorable statement it needs to answer the question, "What is this church all about?"

Keep these parameters in mind:

✓ Is it biblical?

✓ Does it reflect our uniqueness as a church?

✓ Will it serve the long term goals of our members?

✓ Will it appeal to the un-churched?

> "Introducing people to the person, the purpose,
> and the power of Jesus Christ."

In attempting to put their vision into words many churches end up coming across sounding too vague and generalistic; or they try to be too inclusive, wanting to try to be all things to all people; or they succeed at being clever and poetic, but don't really say anything at all. Imagine that a totally unchurched (and hopefully unbiased) visitor attends your service. When asked afterwards if he enjoyed it he might well say, "It was nice! I enjoyed the music, the message was helpful, and you all seem very passionate. It was a nice meeting. But what exactly is it that you people do?" Every member of your church needs to be able to answer that question quickly, simply and forcefully.

A community service organization might also have a good club meeting, but when asked that question any member would quickly be able to say, "We build children's hospitals." Or perhaps, "We fund cancer research." Or maybe, "We fight AIDS in Africa."

Purpose asks, "Why?"

Vision asks, "What?"

Strategy asks, "How?"

Goals ask, "When?"

Remember, Jesus never told us to go into all the world and have nice services! He sent us to bring "glad tiding of great joy to all people"; to change the world one life at a time; to set captives free, shake up cities, transform nations, and not to stop until he comes back! When you take such a radical purpose and condense it to fit into your neighbourhood it should become even more powerful. We show people how to dream, live the dream, and then dream again! We save marriages, rebuild ruined lives, and teach people how to win at the game of life. We are there to rescue the perishing, right the wrongs, and build lives worth living!

A well-crafted vision statement should be:

1. Crisp: not too long, not too short. Avoid repetition and redundancy.

2. Creative: make it fresh and creative versus stale or clichéd.

3. Clear: try to avoid words that are ambiguous or have other interpretations.

4. Contemporary: use terminology that is culturally relevant for your situation today.

Taking into account everything above, put your vision into words:

_____

_____

_____

Create A Tag Line

Now you can further edit your vision statement down to a phrase of no more than about five or six words – something that can fit on a T-shirt or coffee mug but still capture the heart of your church's mission.

Slogans and tag lines will change over time, but should always grow out of a similar process to insure that they truly reflect the vision of the church. Your tag line eventually comes to be associated with your name in people's minds so make sure it's what you want them to think of you.

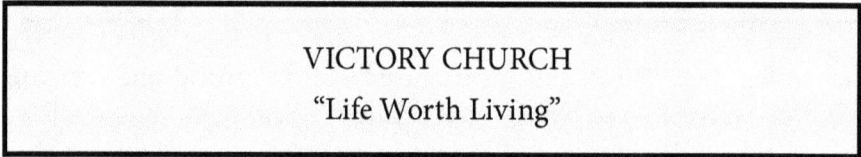

VICTORY CHURCH

"Life Worth Living"

Can you think of any other popular tag lines?

1 Panasonic: "Just slightly ahead of our time"

2 McDonalds: "I'm loving it"

3 _____

4 _____

5 _____

6 _____

7 _____

8 _____

9 _____

Communicating Vision

Once you have done the work of defining the vision that God has for you, then you must begin the never-ending task of communicating the vision. You need to understand that something isn't communicated when it is written down or printed on a banner. Nor is it communicated once you've preached it or shared it. It is communicated only when the core group "gets it!" When they own it, run with it, and share it with others – then you've communicated it. So implanting the vision in the hearts of your core group, and eventually into the whole church, isn't an event – it's an ongoing process. There are a couple of reasons for this:

Firstly, while a vision may be fairly simple to define or state, in order to really be grasped it will have to be interpreted for people. In other words, you might state your vision as "Loving God & Loving Others", just for example.

But in order for people to really understand it and buy into it, they need to know what that means to them. What will they have to do to help fulfill that vision? Does loving God mean that they will have to speak in tongues? What will their children have to do? How much will it cost them to help build this vision? How much of their time will they be expected to contribute? What opportunities for personal growth and promotion will be available for those who really pitch in? Will they have to evangelize their neighbours? What will happen if they try and fail at their contribution to the overall effort?

These and a thousand other questions and concerns must be addressed in order for people to understand and "own" the church's vision. That's what we mean by interpretation. Much of your work as a leader is helping your core team to understand and apply the vision to their lives. This takes lots of dialogue and time. It presumes approachability on your part and openness to people's honest questions.

But the time you invest pouring your vision into the hearts of your core team is always well spent. Because once they "own it", they will be the ones who pour it into others and so on and so on.

The second reason that you will always need to communicate vision is because vision grows, changes, and evolves over time. With every goal reached, new goals must be set. As new people join the church, new leadership opportunities and ministry possibilities are added to the multi-faceted work of the church. None of us has the prescience to be able to see every detail of the finished product that the church could eventually become. God may have the final product in his mind but it is only ever revealed to us in progressive phases. On top of that, changing circumstances in the community may necessitate a shift in the vision from time to time. Maybe a large factory or a mine that hires a significant proportion of the city's workers closes down. Suddenly the needs of your community have changed – and if the church wishes to remain effective, it will have to shift its focus too.

This doesn't mean abandoning your original vision, but it needs to be flexible enough to evolve and stay 'sighted-in' on the present needs of the target community. And then the new emphasis will need to be communicated, communicated, and communicated - until people are able to see it, interpret into their own lives and live it out in united effort.

The most important people in a new church plant are the members of the planting team. The senior leader provides the leadership and the overall direction for the plant, but it is the members of the planting team who will do most of the work. It is the team who will do most of the praying for the new church. It is they who will have the most contact with prospective attendees. It is the team who in large part will set the tone and determine the personality of the church.

Suffice to say that these are important people who must be selected with care and managed with skill.

Choosing A Planting Team

Certain key ministry positions must be filled prior to the launching of services, such as worship leaders and musicians, children's workers, and youth workers. Other helpful people include those who can serve as greeters, ushers, sound technicians, computer operators, and so on. In certain special situations there may also be a need for some very special helpers like a chef, an architect, a bus driver, or a pilot. The sooner these individuals can be chosen and begin working together, the better the teamwork can become prior to the Launch Day. People from the community can also join the church during the pre-launch phase, but should be added to the team cautiously, as they may have personal motivation to join a new church in the neighbourhood and end up working at cross-purposes to the team.

These key individuals will form the leadership/planning team for the first many months following the launch, and possibly form the long-term leadership of the church. As God brings in other qualified people they too must be given the opportunity to rise into positions of leadership. Great care must be exercised in selecting these individuals.

Most of the problems encountered in the first year of a new church originate with the planting team.

Look for people who:

✓ Have a proven gifting in the areas you need

✓ Have a proven character and track record

✓ Someone you can work with in a team relationship

Team members should be experienced with a proven character and track record. These are best drawn from known churches where they have served faithfully. You are better off with solid, faithful but less gifted individuals than with highly gifted but unreliable ones. Choose team members carefully!

3.5 LEADING YOUR TEAM

In addition to being a visionary, an entrepreneur, and a jack-of-all-trades, a church planter is also the senior leader and pastor of his leadership team. In many cases the team will include Bible college students and pastoral trainees who will need on-the-job coaching and mentoring as they work with you to plant the church. Others may be just good faithful people who unexpectedly encounter a family crisis in the middle of a launch campaign. If the team God has given you are going to be an asset and help you launch a great church, then they will need to be well organized, well pastored, and well-trained to staff the needs of the church. This means that before you ever end up leading a large church anywhere, you are going to have to successfully lead your core team.

Building Unity

You can start by building and maintaining unity in the team. Unity starts with purpose. In the launching of a new church the planter must have a clear vision of the church's purpose and make every effort to implant that vision in his core group. The more clearly they see your vision, the more closely they will share the same vision. You must protect the church from individuals or other influences that could sabotage the unity of the church. In a new church plant it is common for displaced Christians to join themselves to the work in the hope of gaining a position of influence – getting in on the ground floor, so to speak. The planter must be discerning of people's motives and deal firmly with those who might endanger the work.

Building Momentum

Secondly you need to create, monitor, and maintain the momentum of the team. The dictionary definition is: mass x velocity = momentum. In physics class we all learned that a locomotive at rest can be immobilized by a six inch block of wood under its wheels – but at 70 mph it can crash through a six foot wall of concrete. That's momentum! A related principle is the law of inertia.

Isaac Newton described it as "the tendency of a body at rest to remain at rest, and the tendency of a body in motion to remain in motion." If it is a church "body" we're talking about here, then the implications are clear! The best way to get somewhere is to be in motion. You need to be able set things in motion, generate more momentum, and keep things moving. Once things grind to a halt it can be extremely difficult to get them moving again. Things that kill momentum include:

✓ Complacency and lack of direction

✓ Poor organization and lack of professionalism

✓ Negative attitudes

✓ Politics and power games

✓ Disunity in leadership

If you do everything in your power to prevent these things from affecting the core group, then the natural momentum of an exciting new project will help keep things moving forward. Good leaders continually monitor the momentum of their team, looking for any detractors that must be eliminated, and seeking for ways to increase and strengthen the forward motion of the group. Things that can really build momentum include:

1. A worthwhile vision that is shared by all. The more they share your vision, the more they will share your passion for it. When they see what you see, they will think, speak, work, and sacrifice like you do.

2. A trust bond between leaders and people. A team that likes each other, likes their leader, and like what they're doing, automatically generates the enthusiasm and energy that can build momentum exponentially.

3. Opportunity for real involvement and achievement. Everybody wants to change the world. Here's your chance!

4. Visible progress towards achievable goals. This is why it's important to celebrate milestones and anniversaries in the church. Achieving important steps in the vision gives everyone a renewed sense of commitment to "press on the summit."

5. The manifestation of God's presence and working. This is the ultimate measure of success. The unmistakeable evidence of transformed lives and miraculous interventions encourages everyone that we are on the right track, "Let's put the pedal to the metal!"

Building And Maintaining Leaders

If a church is to achieve long-term sustained growth, the senior pastor must see his main occupation as one of equipping leaders. Yes, he must make sure that people are receiving the pastoral care they need, but unless he can develop and release other leaders to work with him, the scope of his abilities will always remain limited. He must learn to see beyond personality issues and recognize leadership potential in those around him.

Here is a quick guide to identifying potential leaders

(Rate from 1 = extremely poor to 10 = excellent)

What kind of influence do they have on others? How strong is it?

The higher the level of leadership, the higher the level of self-discipline required. Do they have self-restraint? Initiative? Persistence?

Check out their track record. Look for patterns of behaviour that indicate giftings, maturity, areas of weakness, etc.

How are their people skills? Remember – the church is primarily a people business!

Do they have the ability to spot problems and solve them under their own initiative?

Are they a "mover/shaker" type or do they seem content with the status quo?

Are they people who can keep the bigger picture in view at all times or do they seem to get bogged down in details and petty problems?

How are their communication skills? Do they seem able to articulate their thoughts so that others can understand them? Do they seem to "live in their own little world"?

How would you rate their ability to handle stress?

What about their prevailing attitude? Do they carry themselves in a positive spirit? Are they an encouragement to others?

You must continually equip others for leadership. The more leaders you develop the more ministry can be accomplished without anyone "burning out" from overwork and under-appreciation! There are countless books, philosophies, and aids available to help develop leaders. The important thing is to do it! Most recognize a basic four-step process.

1. Have them with you to observe while you are doing things. The best teaching times happen "in the field". Keep a mental list of work that needs to be done and people who could possibly do it. Bring them alongside you. Let them see how you do things. Explain the how's and why's of what you do as you work.

2. Get them to help you while you are doing things. Allow them to get their hands on things with you. You carry the responsibility but they can certainly help you do it.

3. Help them while they do things. Here you trade places – they do it while you help them. Continue to coach and advise them until they get the hang of it. Make sure they understand clearly what you want to accomplish and why. Communicate expectations, timeframes, and what resources they will need to work with.

4. Observe them while they are doing things. They take over the work and just report to you on their progress. Your role now is to encourage and coordinate. You continue to hold them accountable for fulfilling their responsibilities, but you hand over the reins and let them drive. To complete this training cycle, insist that they bring someone else alongside to be their trainee.

If you do this process with your core team, you will set in motion a leadership development culture within the church that will ensure that the church never lacks the leadership it needs to move forward with its vision. Paul instructed Timothy to "teach faithful men who will teach others also."

3.6 CHOOSING FACILITIES AND LOCATIONS

By at least one definition a church is group of people meeting together to worship Jesus. No matter what other forms a church may take it's hard to avoid the need to meet together as a group! And that means finding suitable facilities. Over the years we have launched new congregations in everything from traditional church buildings - complete with steeple, to store-fronts, to banquet halls, to curling rinks, to shopping centres, to schools. Wherever you end up meeting, facilities must be consistent with the church's vision. You can't put a soup kitchen in an office tower. First, work out what the style and vision of the church will be, and then look for a facility that will reinforce and facilitate that vision. Traditionally styled churches should look for community centres, schools, hotels, or church buildings. Street churches will work best in a store front or warehouse type building near their target area. A singles church could meet in a bar, café, or health club.

With a little imagination almost anything can be put to use for the work of the Gospel. In any case there are some firm criteria that a potential building must meet:

1. It must be able to house the ministries of the church. That means space for family worship times that is acoustically workable; plus space for children's classes of different age groups, including a nursery room for babes and toddlers. Calculate your space needs at approximately ten square feet per person. For instance a 1,000 sq ft room can comfortably hold about 100 people including platform area and walkways. In addition to that you will need space for children's classes and nursery. If nothing is available consider renting office space for all mid-week activities and hold services in a local hotel/ convention centre, community hall, club, or school.

2. Facilities must be readily accessible and as visible in the community as possible. A well placed building is a 24 hour/day advertisement for the church. Locate on a main thoroughfare if possible, if not, consider how you can make it easier to find. Just off a main street might be fine as long as you are allowed to put a big sign out on the main intersection that points people to the church. Good signage is vital.

Check local sign by-laws and go as big and beautiful as you can.

3. Adequate parking. Check zoning restrictions for your area, the rule is to get as much parking as you possibly can. If you can't get enough on site, try to strike an agreement with neighbouring properties that may be closed for business when the church is open.

4. Facilities must be attractive. Aim for excellence – many people will judge your church on the appearance of the facility alone. Pay attention to clean and spacious washrooms. Don't reject a building simply because it is run down – a little paint and elbow grease can often work wonders. But be careful not to take on any more of a renovation project than your group can handle within a short period of time. You can continue to upgrade and improve the facility as often as finances will allow.

5. Research local building and zoning requirements before investing any money. There have been cases of churches purchasing a piece of property only to find that zoning restrictions, obstructive neighbours, or even hazardous waste on the property prevented them from being able to develop it. This can be a financial disaster for a church!

Facility options essentially boil down to one of these three: purchase, lease, or rental. The deciding factor in some cases will be availability, in others it will be the cost. A good budgeting guideline is:

✓ 1/3 for facilities

✓ 1/3 for salaries

✓ 1/3 for programs

Within the Victory Churches International family, all local churches contribute ten percent of their general income – a tithe – towards the funding of new church plants and missions projects. This is administrated by the national Head Office.

Taking Your Church Through A Building Project

There are great benefits to owning your facility. The accumulation of equity and control of your budget are substantial considerations. The convenience of having exclusive use of the facility is enticing after months or years of moving equipment, setting up and tearing down for every service, and getting 'bumped' by other groups.

Owning your facility can also generate a feeling of ownership in the congregation and strengthen commitments to the church.

There is some advantage to long-term stability in the same location – you really get to know your neighbours and can become integrated into the community resulting in many evangelistic opportunities. And when you are the owner there is always a possibility of augmenting the budget through rentals and/or sub-letting the facility to other groups in the community. Ownership also gives you the right to have a say in municipal matters that are before city council.

But with ownership come some risks as well. Pressuring people to give during a building fund raising drive can cast a negative veil over the church if it is not managed well. Disagreement over building-related issues can cause serious division in the congregation because they all share such a deep commitment. Down the road the lack of easy mobility can hamper a growing congregation. And even further down the road a dwindling congregation may find that the carrying costs are just too high and a highly specialized church building may not be easy to sell.

The good news is that many churches have been down the "building" road before you. Designing the building with an eye to eventual resale keeps that door unlocked whether the church outgrows it or the congregation shrinks. There are professional church fund-raising ministries that can help a church to implement a successful drive to raise the necessary finances. In general though, it's wise to try and raise as much as possible up front. Don't jump into any project too quickly – make sure that the church is really in agreement and financially prepared for contingencies. Be cautious of a building project that will raise the church's monthly carrying costs by more than 25%. There are lots of financing options to consider. Shop for financing – not all lending institutions are the same.

Don't be afraid to negotiate. Remember – a mortgage will saddle the church with financial obligation for many years to come. And don't give in to the temptation to cut corners on legal advice. A healthy and growing church takes many years of hard work to build and only one foolish mistake to totally destroy!

So we've already got a lot of things prepared and now you're ready to begin the launch process. There are basically two different ways to start new churches. One is just to build incrementally from a small group. The planter (and team) move into the area and gradually build up the church through word-of-mouth and personal contacts. In this approach it is likely that the whole team will have to find a job and support themselves and their families while the church grows. The focus is on winning the lost and personal discipleship. There is nothing wrong with this approach and many fine churches began this way. However, most of what we've shared in this book is geared toward the utilization of a launch event. This approach does most of its preparation behind the scenes and then goes public with a big, well promoted opening day designed to draw as many new people as possible. What they find on that day is a well-organized, fully serviced new church with a plan to quickly assimilate people and establish them in membership.

This essentially involves a promotional campaign that will result in the maximum number of attendees on Launch Day. But first let's talk about advertising. Many sincere Christians harbour an antipathy towards advertising the church. I once heard someone say of a well-known evangelical church that their use of a neon sign on their property was proof that they were a cult! Some assume that if God wants people to come to church then he will bring them there himself. The problem with this kind of thinking is that it totally contradicts what the Bible tells us.

If God was planning to just sovereignly fill churches then why did Jesus say, "Go into all the world and preach the Gospel to every creature"? It is clear that Christ was depending on his followers to spread the news by every means possible. In his day that was limited to word-of-mouth and personal letters, but today we have many more types of advertising media at our disposal. In fact, Jesus himself used advertising! We read in Luke 10:1 that, "The Lord appointed 70 others also, and sent them out two by two before his face into every city and place where he himself was about to go."

These 70 were forerunners – sent ahead to spread the news and prepare things for Christ's arrival. That is one reason why crowds lined the roads when Jesus began to enter a city – they knew he was coming!

Although great worship, evangelism, and discipleship are indispensable to a healthy church, without good marketing no one knows you're doing it! Your services may be life-changing, but without some kind of promotion most of the people who need life-transformation simply won't even know you're there. A good church is one of the greatest things in the world. Certainly churches have their problems from time to time, but when it's all working the way it should, it's awesome! It's a fantastic, fun, fulfilling place to be. But in too many cases it's also the best kept secret in the world! We might be surprised how many people would love to join in, if they only knew what they were missing.

Marketing puts you in control of your church's public image. You can rest assured that the community will form an opinion of your new church. Without a marketing plan they may be completely unaware of your presence. Or worse, they may actively spread vicious rumours about it being a weird cult. If you do nothing to help shape the public's perception of your church, you can be sure that the Devil will. If people are going to form an opinion anyway, then you can help them to form the opinion you prefer by taking charge of the image that the church presents to the community. You do that through advertising.

First, to borrow some advertising terminology, you need to define your product. This isn't as straight-forward as it seems. There are many "products" that your church could legitimately offer. If your target prospect were to ask, "Why should I go to your church? What will I get out of it?" The answer you give would be close to defining your "product". It doesn't take long to realize that "Receiving eternal life" or "Finding the answers to life's questions" or similar truths are far too vague and too large of a topic to induce many people to come and check it out for themselves. Then what is the product? Is it a worship experience? Is it a wholesome pastime for families?

Fortunately we have already done some work in a previous section to determine what will be your church's values and vision. If you've completed that process then you have already sat down with your key leaders and compiled a mission statement that passes the "T-Shirt" test for advertising and promotional purposes. Condensing all that a church stands for down to an accurate but marketable tag line is no simple task. But once you've done it you have come a long way towards defining your "product" and answering the question, "What's in it for me?" Your vision statement should satisfy these four factors:

1. Is it the will and purpose of God?

2. Does it reflect the particular strengths of your church/pastor?

3. Will it serve the long-term needs of growing church families?

4. Does it appeal to the needs of the non-churched?

Once you have identified your product you can plan to use it in many different ways: in pictures, signs, posters, newsprint, spoken messages, business cards, internet videos, and more. The problem isn't finding a suitable advertising medium; it's narrowing down the multiplicity of different mediums to the ones that you can manage with your budget. No matter what media you utilize, what you want to be able achieve in a launch campaign is a continual "top-of-mind-awareness" of the church in the community.

Whatever type of media you decide to use, you must always strive for excellence. Shabby or amateur work tells people that you are a shabby and amateur church regardless of the ad content. Route all church promotions through a qualified commercial artist. Normally there is someone in or connected to the team who can lend some expertise in this crucial area. Make sure to insist on clear, simple layouts versus cluttered, complicated ones: a maximum two different fonts on a page, and so on. Develop recognizable themes, artwork, and styles, and let them evolve slowly enough for it to be readily recognizable. Don't invest a pile of time and money developing a visual style for the church and then change it all next month.

Here are some things that can really pay off. When it comes to getting great advertising value for your dollar, nothing beats a mobile street-level sign. These are readily rentable, but if your local sign laws allow you to use it as much as you like, then it's worth it to buy your own.

Typically about eight feet by five feet and planted right in front of your facility, these big signs instantly give people your location, service information, and an impression of what you're all about. Being at eye-level for drivers makes them easy to see. And because commuters are people of habit, they will see it again and again as they travel past your place on their way to work every day. A clever quote can stick with them long after they've seen it. Make sure that you change it at least once a month so that its familiarity doesn't make it invisible after a while. Other types of visual advertising media include billboards, sandwich board signs, flyers, handbills, posters, newspaper ads, public service announcements, and banners.

> **Nine out of ten people today will not visit a church until they have first visited its website.**

One of the most important forms of advertising these days is a good website. Nine out of ten people will not attend your church until they have first visited your website or Facebook page. Their reasoning is that the more they can find out about you before they venture through your doors, the less chance of having an unpleasant experience or being embarrassed having their friends find out they went to a weird church. Long before Launch Day you should have your website up and running and the web address featured prominently on all your publications and promotions.

Second to websites, newspapers are still one of the most affordable ways to advertise. Buying display ad space can be expensive, but try the upcoming events column in the classifieds. Or better yet, be your own reporter. Take photos of everything and anything the church does, write up a report of church activities, and submit it to your local paper. They may or may not use them but they definitely can't if they don't have them. More often than not they are eager to have some local news and will print it for free.

Advertising is a HUGE commercial business and takes a considerable amount of skill to utilize successfully. But when Jesus said, "Go and tell", he put us into the advertising business. If we want to get the Good News out to our world, then we need to become masters of this trade. The possibilities are enormous: radio, TV, cable programs, telephone campaigns, and door-to-door drives are only the beginning. Be creative – you've got lots of competition! There are many ways besides normal advertising media that can get you noticed.

What about hosting events like seminars, free food day in the park, theatrical productions, hosting sports tournaments, or getting yourself invited to be the guest expert on a radio talk show? All of these and many more are primarily ways to raise your church's profile in the community.

Use your building to advertise. If you have a permanent location, your building is a big, beautiful, 24 hour-a-day advertisement for the church! First make sure that you choose a visible location, one that people can't miss on their daily commute. Then paint it attractively and put a big sign on it. From then on it is free advertising. Consider using your facility to host or rent space out to community groups and events. This probably won't get anyone saved, but for most people the biggest step in joining your church is the first one – stepping into your building. Once they've been there for other activities, and looked around at your internal promotions and take-away information – they will be just that much more prepared to come when they are invited to a service.

Many churches perpetually struggle to grow and to have sufficient funds to operate from month to month. Part of the problem is that it is too easy to become inwardly focused on the needs of the members and allow that to become the overwhelming priority of the church's ministry. Certainly people need to be looked after. But the secret of abundant finances is continual growth. Most churches would be well advised, whether just launching or long since launched, to allocate a much bigger portion of their budget to good advertising. It is an investment in the evangelism of your community and the future progress of the church.

Having said that, there are many ways to be visible on a limited budget. Promote multiple events on one flyer and distribute them yourself. Find out when the local newspaper discounts its regular rates in order to fill empty spaces each week. Alert the television, radio stations, and newspapers when you hold a news-worthy event. They can't cover it if they don't know it's happening! Shop around: from sign painters to interest rates there is always a competitor who is willing to offer a better deal! Challenge your congregation to give towards big advertising projects – you might be surprised!

Don't be discouraged if the whole city doesn't stampede your church the first time you place a classified ad. Be prepared to invest and wait for long term results. Media visibility is a long term, seed-bed type of strategy. Good advertising creates receptivity to all your outreach programs. When teams go door to door it's always better to hear, "Oh yes, I've heard of you" than to hear, "Never heard of you. Slam!" Budget for it on an annual basis and strive to increase your budget yearly.

Designing An Advertising Campaign

An advertising campaign could and should involve a variety of different types of media. Multiple exposures to your ads will help create top-of-mind-awareness all the more rapidly. But you should select one as the main approach, leaving other forms of media to play a support role. For example, you could decide to make a telephone campaign your main strategy. Flyers, newspaper ads, and such could all support that with a teaser like: "We'll be calling you!" Whatever methods you decide to utilize, everything should be geared towards Launch Day. The idea is build anticipation and make people wait until then to check the church out. If people attend a service during the pre-launch phase there won't be much to impress them or bring them back for more. But a big opening day with hundreds of people there is enormously exciting for everyone and is a fantastic incentive for people to plug right in and make it their regular Sunday habit!

You will have to begin by estimating the costs of various methods and then choose which approaches would work best in your situation:

✓ Mass mail:

Farm an area by blanketing it with bulk mail flyers several times over. This is a fairly economical way to reach a lot of people. A well-designed flyer in every mailbox ensures that most people in your target area are aware of the big Launch Day. Plan to use a mail-drop per home per week for at least three weeks (four/five is better). Content of the flyers should inform people about the church's beliefs and programs but point everything to the Launch Day. Attractively designed flyers/brochures/cards can draw many people to the church and will continue to work long after Launch Day.

✓ Telephone:

Develop a prospect list through telephone solicitation and follow up with mail-outs. This is also fairly economical, but telemarketing is sometimes prohibited or at least frowned upon these days. Normally you will target a specific area and obtain all the phone numbers for that area. Then assemble a telephone team who can put in about six hours/day (mornings & evenings). Provide a script for each caller to use and train them how to handle different kinds of calls. Interested respondents are mailed a series of informational invitations. Again, all materials point people to Launch Day. In responding to people's questions about the church, try to leave enough unanswered that they will feel compelled to visit in order to truly satisfy their curiosity. "You know… the best way is to just come and see for yourself."

✓ Billboard campaign:

Utilize a number of billboards or other large display ads to promote opening day. This can be quite expensive but certainly gets attention. Large display ads can be found on bus stop shelters, buildings, free-standing billboards, bus signs, bridges, and all kinds of places.

✓ Electronic campaign:

In today's world of electronic media more and more of our news and other information comes to us via television, radio, and increasingly the internet and social media of all kinds. You may reach the older generation with newspaper advertising, but if you want to connect with young couples and young adults you need to mount a social media campaign. This involves having a top rate website for them to visit, but it also means using Facebook, Twitter, Instagram, and other such forums to network and build a following. This can be a powerful tool. But the difference between social media and other forms of visual media is significant. What works in one may completely backfire in the other.

"We are now in a 'digital communication culture'. It is not just that the tools we use to communicate are different. The very way that we communicate, even think, is changing. Len Sweet's book "Viral: How Social Networking Is Poised to Ignite Revival", explains this quantum leap. These are key elements of social media:

- relational and personal, not anonymous and generalized
- dialogue and discussion, not proclamation and preaching
- widespread use of the visual – photos and videos
- frequently accessed 24/7 on mobile phones, not computers

Since Biblical evangelism is usually relational and discussion-based, social media is an ideal match."

www.internetevangelismday.com

The reason for this is simple: visual media is primarily selling an event to anonymous strangers; social media is participating in an ongoing dialogue with friends. Before you can use social media to promote your Launch Day you will have to spend a lot of lead time developing a network who want to hear what you have to say. This involves real conversational skills as opposed to normal advertising talents like graphic layout. Again, think relationship instead of audience.

Getting too "preachy" or only ever pushing events will quickly alienate much of your network. Instead, aim to participate in their lives on a long term basis and every so often add a comment or a link to points them to a relevant resource. The objective is to pique their interest in learning more, not shut them down by winning theological debates!

Whatever approach you choose, remember - people's attention span is only so long. Ideally the campaign should last between four and six weeks. Less time than that and many people won't even notice your advertising nor have time to plan on attending. More time than that and they may just lose interest after waiting so long.

The launching of a new church is one of the best evangelism methods there is. In fact, it may well be the best chance the church will ever have to draw in completely unchurched people and see them make a commitment to Christ. The importance of taking full advantage of this reality cannot be over-stated. People like to check out something new, and new churches are no exception. Many people have 'pre-judged' that church isn't for them without even attending a single service at a church like yours. Chances are, if you could just convince them to come once, they would really enjoy it. Over the years I've heard many first-time visitors say, "I didn't know it was like this. I like this!" Generally speaking, people are most likely to show up through an invitation from someone they know. But the chances of them agreeing to come with their friend are at least twice as good when it is the grand opening of something brand new. Work as hard as you can to get such un-churched attendees out for Launch Day. Many will turn out to be long term joiners.

The most successful growing churches are the ones that have truly made evangelism a vital component of their purpose. Of course they still offer every kind of program to meet the needs of mainstream Christian families, but through it all pulses a heartbeat for souls. This means it's a normal part of the planning and programming dialogue, it shows up regularly in preaching illustrations, it is the specific purpose of many programs and events, it is promoted through small groups, and it is seamlessly integrated into their vision in every way possible.

It means that the church is prepared to handle new converts.

Provision is made for introducing new kids into children's programs at any time. Processes for identifying visitors and integrating them into the fellowship are well thought out and well-used. Baptismal services and discipleship classes are a normal part of the weekly event schedule. In other words, they believe in evangelism, they embrace evangelism, they are prepared for evangelism, and they do evangelism.

This kind of extended focus takes a firm hand on the wheel, so to speak. It is the most natural thing in the world for new churches to put lots of effort into outreach in order to get launched. But as soon as they are up and running they can easily become preoccupied with getting their new house in order. There are people to get to know, departments to staff, procedures to work out, facilities to renovate, and a host of other vital concerns that need to be addressed. If they are not careful, they can quickly become absorbed in these never-ending maintenance issues and unconsciously push evangelism to the back burner.

Before long the inward-focussed busyness becomes a habit and the habit will eventually become the personality of the new church. People get comfortable with their new circle of relationships and evangelism just dies of neglect. The senior leader needs to understand this all-too-typical trend and maintain a constant emphasis on reaching out to the lost for at least the first 18 months. This will ensure that a passion for evangelism becomes a deep-rooted part of the personality of the new church. From there on evangelism will be natural, effortless, and continually fruitful from season to season.

3.9 LAUNCH DAY CHECKLIST:

✓ Ensure that facilities are clean and decorated appropriately – you only get a chance to do the opening day of a new church once! Make it a celebration!!!

✓ Have people prepared to oversee greeting, ushering, nursery, and children's ministry and to run their program regardless of how many show up. You have to demonstrate that you are ready for bigger numbers.

✓ Appoint a photographer to record the whole day, from pre-service prayer, to the worship team in action, every speaker and lots of shots of the crowd before, during and after. These will be invaluable in putting names to faces as quickly as possible in the weeks following.

✓ Make sure that everyone gets an information packet including a bulletin and flyers for any up-coming Big Days. You want them to plan on coming back. Your goal is to turn them all into regular attendees!

✓ Have visitor cards ready and make time in the service to get as many filled out as possible. Ask every single person to complete one during a musical special.

✓ Preaching topics should be motivational and topical – geared toward the un-churched. Audio-visual/ aids and drama are always an asset.

✓ Have a well-planned calendar of events to promote in the bulletin and commence all weekly activities the first week. Have several different affinity groups that people can check out in the first week: ladies morning break, men's breakfast, youth, kids club, home groups, mid-week service, membership classes, etc.

✓ Announce a special organizational meeting for anyone who would like to get involved in the church to be held that Sunday evening or Monday night. This doesn't mean that you put them into leadership positions right away or at all. But those interested may prove to be the most qualified candidates. Start them with a membership course and then ongoing leadership training. Over time you will be able to see who is best suited to begin stepping into longer term roles of leadership within the church.

✓ End the service earlier than normal and provide refreshments and visiting time for everyone. Make sure your leaders meet as many people as possible and stay as long as people want to visit.

Sample Service Format

9:00 Pre-service band warm up

9:30 Pre-service prayer (15 min). Get all greeters in place by 9:45

10:00	Praise – upbeat, up tempo choruses. Start promptly.
10:10	Welcome by Pastor, distribute visitor cards & pencils
10:13	Special song, ushers collect visitor cards
10:20	Worship
10:35	Announcements/offering
10:40	Dramatization
10:45 ministry	Release children to children's church, Message/
11:30	Close service, coffee & fellowship

The First Week

1. Collect all visitor cards and names of all attendees and follow them up

a. Phone each one every week until they are confirmed

2. Mail a Launch Day Newsletter reporting on how it went to every mail contact whether they attended or not

3. Hold an organizational meeting with all those interested. Take the opportunity to:

a. Share the church's vision and values

b. Answer questions about the church

c. Find out what people are interested in doing and enlist their help

The First Month

1. Every attendee from Launch Day and all other contacts should have been called at least twice and visited by someone from the church

2. Membership and leadership training should be well under way

3. New leaders should be in place in the core ministries of the church

4. Regular weekly evangelism should be under way

The First Year

1. Be prepared to lose many of your original leaders. Often people join a new church plant for personal reasons and move on when they fail to realize their agenda.

2. Keep reaching out to the lost. In the long run those you reach and disciple will prove to be your greatest asset. Keep the focus of the church strongly on evangelism for at least the first 18 months.

3. Keep your eyes on the church's momentum. The excitement of Launch Day doesn't last forever. You need to be incorporating new people and staying fresh with programs and activities to keep up the speed.

4. Spend all the time you can to develop a strong, committed leadership core. The Piretto Principle: Spend 80% of your time with 20% of your people.

5. If you had to start in weekly rental facilities you may be in a good position after the first year to settle the church in a more permanent location.

SECTION 4
After You Plant

Statistics tell us that new churches tend to have a high mortality rate. Many don't survive past their third year. Perhaps the timing was wrong. Or the church was started for the wrong reasons. It's not surprising to find that most of these cases there were problems with the leader – financial hardship, conflict with the other core leaders, moral failure, or just discouragement.

The best insurance against such a disappointing finish is to be aware of the challenges that lie ahead and to be prepared for them. The thrill and excitement of Launch Day quickly turns into the demanding work of assimilating people and establishing a fully functioning church.

4.1 TURNING THE CROWD INTO A CONGREGATION

When most new churches begin they must first be like a hospital; then a family, then a training center, and finally an army. When people come in the door, very few of them want to do anything. Many of them have been hurt and they distrust leadership. To try to get any kind of major commitment from them will drive many of them out.

That's a mistake that a lot of church planters make. They try to get all new people to be committed instantly. But that's not wisdom. Instead of trying to get them committed and coming out to everything, you need to love them. Teach how-to messages – hospital messages. You can teach discipleship training messages to your core group; but speak differently to the Sunday crowd until they become a congregation. Teach them how to overcome fear and rejection. Teach on forgiveness and how they can be released from resentment. They need to know how to love and trust again. Help them to repair their past so they can get up and go on! And just because people have been highly involved in the past doesn't mean they are ready to do it again. Many of them just need to be loved and accepted unconditionally; as we do this and continue to put value into them by speaking words of life to their potential, they'll become strong enough to once again make a fresh commitment to the work of the Lord.

Three months after we launched one new church we put involvement sheets through the congregation to see what areas of ministry people wanted to be involved in. When they came back, only seven out of over 300 people had filled them out. Very few people wanted to make any kind of real commitment to any area of ministry. Many of them used to be elders, deacons, worship leaders and even pastors. But they were in an unhealthy spiritual and emotional condition and had no desire to be involved in any kind of ministry. They needed to be in the intensive care ward, not up on the platform or making decisions on how the church was going to be run. After ministering to the people for one year, we put involvement sheets through the church again, and almost every one of them was returned to us with the people wanting to be involved! By this time the church had become a spiritual family, so we began extensive training programs to move the church into the army stage. Looking back over the situation, we can see how God gave us great wisdom!

When the crowds come in, we must begin by finding out who we have, and where they are at, spiritually, emotionally, mentally and socially (Luke 2:52).

And everyone who was in distress, everyone who was in debt and everyone who was discontent gathered to him. So he became captain over them. (1 Samuel 22:2)

The 3D Church

King David had what has been called a '3D' church when he began. Many new churches start with those who are discontent, in distress and in debt. And you will find that many have been disengaged from a local church for a while.

If this is the case, the pastor must begin by teaching what I call hospital messages; messages that do not require them to do anything as far as helping in the church. They are messages that focus on getting them well and out of hospital and back to work.

Messages such as:

- How to forgive and forget

- How to turn their setbacks into spring boards

- How to trust again and open themselves up to new relationships

- How to become emotionally stable and handle stress and pressure

- How to walk in love

- How to study the Word and apply it in practical ways in their lives

> 90% of those interviewed said the senior pastor played a key role in their decision to stay and join:
> ✓ Preaching that teaches the Bible
> ✓ Preaching that applies to my life
> ✓ Authenticity of the pastor: "the pastor is a real person"
> ✓ Pastor's conviction: conviction and surety of knowing truth
> ✓ Personal contact by the pastor (1/3 said this was crucial)
> ✓ Pastor is a good communicator
> ✓ Pastor is a good leader

When people have recovered sufficiently, they want to leave the hospital and return to work.

The process goes like this: first, a hospital, then a family, then a training center and finally an army. We take wounded soldiers off the front lines and get them healed as quickly as possible so we can get them back into active service.

Hospital churches never grow very big; because the people are high maintenance, low impact Christians. The objective is to minister the Gospel in such a way that the people are delivered and restored to health as quickly as possible. Then train them to become active members in the church.

We try to bring people to the place where they become low maintenance, high impact Christians. Where they know how to feed themselves, pray for themselves and use their gifts to do for others what has been done for them. The type of people you have in your congregation is similar to that which you are likely to attract.

If you've got high maintenance Christians, chances are that's the kind of people you're going to attract. You have to use great wisdom to turn that around. "Wisdom has built her house; she has hewn out her seven pillars" (Proverbs 9:1). You will need some pillars in the faith to help you reach the lost and then turn them from being high maintenance, low impact Christians into high impact, low maintenance Christians. Jesus took Peter through the process of going from a reed to a stone, to a pillar. Leaders must know what it takes to make a pillar out of a reed. You have to be a pillar person to grow a pillar person! A pillar is one who takes weight and bears responsibility.

One of the most profitable and rewarding things I have ever done is to start a 6 am Tuesday morning men's meeting. It runs for one hour with verse-by-verse exposition through the books of the Bible. I cover a few verses; giving my understanding of the passage and then I ask for comments or questions. I make sure I always cover at least a chapter of the Bible so the men feel like they are getting somewhere. This gives lots of opportunity to have great times of discussion and deal with any potential church problems without singling anybody out because it's just the next verse of scripture.

I always finish the sharing at 7 am, as some men have to go to work, but many of the men try and adjust their schedules so they can stay for breakfast. I always stay for breakfast, and many of the men are still around at 8:30 or even 9 am.

This is the highlight of the week for many of the men, including me – I love it! I get to know the men and they get to know me, and each other better. It also helps me to get to know the Word better because the men make comments and ask questions about the Word, which helps to broaden my knowledge of the Word, thereby enabling me to be better equipped, to help the men apply the Word in their practical situations in life. The men who are regular attendees at this meeting become fully assimilated into the life of the church within a very short period of time. - GSH

One of the first things we need to do is get to know the names of the people. Jesus said, "I know my sheep by name" (John 10:1-4).

We have to know them, grow them and show them how to live a victorious Christian life.

You should have a church list made up of members; regular attendees and second time visitors. Point out to your staff which members they must know by name, the regular attendees they should know by name, and the visitors they need to get to know by name.

Have a membership training course that you put people through. A membership course is a way of informing the people what you as a church believe, what your vision is, how you plan on getting there and how they can help if they choose to be part of this family. It's a way of finding out more about the people; and giving the people a chance to find out more about you, who you are, and where you are going.

Those who have been through the membership course and are willing to make a commitment to membership are usually ready for involvement in the local church; and are willing to tithe. The membership course is a part of discipleship training and is a great way to get all of the people in a new church on the same page.

Through the membership course you can find out what people are gifted for, what they have done in the past, and what areas they would like to become involved in. During such a course, we usually put everyone through a few different kinds of tests to help them find out what they are gifted for. Afterwards we recruit them for the different areas of ministry within the church depending on their passion, gifting and ability. We ask them for a short-term, usually a three-month, commitment. If after three months they don't like it, they can get out of it without feeling bad to try another area of ministry that they may be better suited for.

The following five things will help you to determine if a person is fully assimilated into the life of the church. The more of these things that are true about a person, the more they are assimilated into the life of the church.

1. A regular weekly attendee

2. A regular contributor financially

3. Involved in a small group

4. Has an identifiable task

5. Has developed five to ten friendships within the church

Six Keys For Increasing Retention

1. Clear Doctrine

People are on a quest for truth. Preaching that is relevant, unpretentious, and easy to understand always connects. Aim for messages that show people how to live, rather than just show off the skills of the preacher!

2. High Expectations

The research shows churches with high expectations not only reach the unchurched but retain them as well! Communication that church members are expected to live and minister in a way that is consistent with New Testament teachings not only promotes involvement but increases retention.

IMPORTANCE OF FIRST IMPRESSIONS

88% indicated Friendliness in the People was a big factor

44% indicated Nice Facilities/Adequate Space was major

Clean restrooms were deemed essential. The most intense comments came regarding the cleanliness, neatness and safety of nursery, preschool and children's areas

33% indicated Greeters and Welcome Centers were important

31% mentioned the Organization of the Worship Service (orderly or chaotic?)

---

3. An Entry Point Class

You can call it a newcomers class or whatever you wish, but some kind of formal orientation helps answer the newcomer's top question: "How will I fit in here?" Studies show that when a suitable class is provided retention rates soar. And the higher the church's expectations of newcomers participating in such a class, the higher the retention rate after two years.

Required Membership Class - 112%!

(Churches which required people to attend a class not only retained all the original attendees, but actually added more!)

Expected but not required - 89%

Available but not expected or required - 72%

4. Small Groups/Sunday School

The evidence is clear, the un-churched stick to a church when they are actively enrolled in a small group. Five years after joining a church, 83% are still active and attend small groups compared to 16% who simply attend worship services! Small group leadership, however, is a position of great influence with people. Don't rush into establishing these until you have proven leaders that you can really trust.

5. Clarity of Purpose

Churches that are effective at reaching and retaining people are clear about their purpose. A former un-churched person said: "I was attracted to the church because you know where they stand and where they are going."

6. Ministry Involvement

A total of 62% of respondents indicated their ministry involvement was the glue that kept them active in the church. Once you get to know newcomers, don't be afraid to ask them to get involved. People don't really feel a sense of ownership until they are a part of making it happen!

Know What You Are Looking For

In Matthew 10:5-6, Jesus instructed His disciples, "Do not go into the way of the Gentiles, and do not enter city of the Samaritans. But go rather to the lost sheep of the house of Israel." Jesus' instruction narrowed down their target. In the natural, different kinds of bait are required to catch different kinds of fish. The same thing is true spiritually.

Go where the fish are biting. Jesus told his disciples to shake the dust off their feet and move on to another place when the people openly rejected His message. In other words, "If the fish aren't biting in one location, then change locations! Go to where the fish are biting!" Some people simply aren't hungry.

Understand The Mindset Of The People And Their Perceived Needs

To break into a community you have to understand the mindset of the people and what their perceived needs are. The real need is always Jesus, but you have to start with the perceived need and direct them back to the only one that can meet all their real needs – Jesus Christ. One of the best ways to find out what unbelievers are thinking and feeling is to go out and do a survey. Rick Warren in his book, The Purpose Driven Church, said that he started Saddleback Community Church by going door-to-door for 12 weeks and surveying the un-churched in his area. He came up with the following five survey questions, which we as a church planting movement have used on numerous occasions.

1. What do you think is the greatest need in this area? This question gets people to talk to you.

2. Are you actively attending any church?

3. Why do you think most people don't attend church?

4. If you were looking for a church to attend, what kinds of things would you be looking for?

5. What advice can you give to a minister who really wants to help people?

If someone came to my door and asked me these questions, I'd be more than happy to help them with their survey.

After Rick Warren and his team had gathered all the information from the survey, they mailed a letter to the community addressing the major concerns of the un-churched, and at the same time announcing a church service designed to counteract the most common excuses they gave. This strategy has been used by many church planting movements all around the world to help plant new churches. Through the survey, the letter and good pre-service planning; Rick Warren was able to gather 205 people for the first service at Saddleback Community Church.

Why Do Visitors Come Back?

As a rule, the pastor is not the one who attracts first-time visitors. But he is a major reason why visitors come back. A major survey done by Thom S. Rainer, Dean of the Billy Graham School of Mission, Evangelism and Church growth reveals the reasons why visitors come back to a church. The pastors' preaching was top of the list with 90% and doctrine was number two on the list with 88%. That should make every pastor want to pray, study, prepare and preach better so that people would want to come back and hear what they had to say!

Where do visitors come from? They might come because they saw an advertisement in the newspaper or because someone gave them an invitation card. They might come because of your location; you're closer and easier to get to than any other church. They might come because a friend or a relative invited them. There are many reasons why people attend a church for the first time. But one thing is for sure; they won't come back unless there is something about the message, something about the pastor, and something about the church service that can draw them back.

If you are a pastor, you must honestly ask yourself, "What kind of a person am I? Am I a friendly person?" If you're not a friendly person, you're already on the losing end. You have to be friendly! You have to be outgoing! You have to love people!

Some people love the Word and they love to teach, but they don't love people.

The Gospel is a people business. As a leader, you will attract who you are, not who you want. What kind of people do you naturally relate to? What types of people naturally gravitate towards you? What kind of people do you have a hard time understanding? What touches your heart? You'll best reach those you can relate to.

Second-time visitors to the church are hot contacts. If we don't have good, friendly and effective follow-up of these visitors, we will simply let these people slip through the cracks.

Whenever we have planted a church, we put a strong emphasis on the follow up. If people don't come back to our church, it wasn't because they weren't loved. It wasn't that the preaching wasn't exciting.

It wasn't because we didn't have everything in place. And it certainly wasn't because they weren't followed up on. If they didn't come back, it was because they didn't want to attend our church. And that's all right. But never let people leave because of your slothfulness. People need to know how much you care and that you appreciate them making the effort to attend your church.

If you're having a lot of visitors but none of them are staying, ask yourself why. If you don't know why go back to your visitor cards and phone every person and ask them why they didn't come back.

For example:

Hello. This is the pastor (or member of the pastoral team) from the new church. I know you were in our church a few weeks ago, and I just want to ask you one simple question. Don't even think about hurting my feelings. Just tell me the truth. Why haven't you come back to our church again?

Now the natural tendency is to avoid making those kinds of calls, because you don't really want to know the truth. Maybe because they'll say that you had body odour when you hugged them or your breath smelled so bad they didn't want to come back.

Worse still, your preaching was boring. Are you open to honest criticism and instruction? The Bible says if you rebuke a wise man he will love you (Proverbs 9:8).

Be strong and very courageous, go ahead phone and ask people, why? How are you going to find out why people aren't staying in your church if you don't ask them? You can assume they didn't like certain parts of the service, but you don't really know until you ask.

Some things you can change, and some things you can't. But a survey of this kind can be of great assistance in helping you retain more of the future visitors that come to your church.

Making Contacts

Friends and relatives of new converts are warm contacts because you already have something in common. You can say, "Good morning! This is pastor Bob (or a pastoral representative). Your Mom comes to our church." You immediately have something in common. Or, maybe you're from the same country. That can be a good conversation starter. Use that to your advantage as an open door of communication.

Hurting people are usually open for help, no matter where that help may come from. Show them the Gospel. Touch them with the Love of God. Do they have a car that's broken down and needs to be fixed? Phone a mechanic in your church and ask him to go over and fix it. Do they have any food in the cupboard? If not, then take them some food. Take it from your own cupboard first, and then from your congregation. What about those who feel the need for a recovery program?

First-time parents are also in a very vulnerable time. They've never been parents before and don't have a clue what to do. They need much more than misguided books on child-rearing and old wives' tales.

It's a good time to minister to them at their point of need with some biblically-based parenting classes.

Some good teaching on marriage, with Christ at the center, will go a long way in helping engaged couples and newlyweds.

Some pastors get the newspaper and read the obituaries, the births and the marriages. Then, they'll send a card to those people. They'll send a sympathy card to those who have recently lost a loved one. They'll put the church name on it and a handwritten note offering comfort and counselling. If it's for a birth, they'll send a card saying, "Congratulations on your new daughter. Should you need some help, please don't hesitate to call us."

What a wonderful idea! They are in a time and phase of their lives when they're more open to the Gospel than at other times. Others who are open to the Gospel are those who are terminally ill, along with their families, as well as those who have lost their job. Reach out to the hurting. The Gospel is people reaching people with the love of Christ. We're in the people business.

Finally, new residents to the community are open to hear from you. If you have a welcome wagon in your area, start putting Bibles in the welcome wagon, along with bulletins from your church or invitations to your church service. These people are new in town. They're looking for friends and a sense of community. So, reach out to them. Have a good website and make sure all of your literature has your website address on it.

Focus on reaching receptive people. Don't go after green fruit all the time. Non-growing churches focus on re-enlisting inactive people. But God called pastors to catch fish and feed sheep, not to corral goats. So many people spend so much time running after the rebellious and the offended, that they have no time for evangelism. If people leave your church, by all means go and talk to them. But if they don't want to come back, don't spend all your time trying to get them back. Focus on the people who are receptive to the good news of salvation, healing, deliverance, and reconciliation through Christ Jesus.

Social Media

Years ago it was common for pastors to do personal visitation, counselling and praying for people right in their own homes, or just maintaining relationship through social get-togethers. People's need for pastoral care hasn't changed, but our methods of staying in touch certainly have.

The advent of social media and the prevalence of cell phones have changed the way we connect with people, both inside and outside of the church. Personal home visits or phone calls are almost viewed as an invasion of privacy today! Instead people utilize Facebook pages or Twitter to stay in touch. The advantages are that it allows people to be more selective in who and what they wish to talk about. A quick text message or email easily replaces the many hours of arranging, preparing, and travelling that face-to-face meetings require. And people can retain more anonymity – only revealing as much of themselves as they wish. All of these factors have helped fuel a world-wide revolution in how we form communities and live out relationships.

Any minister who lacks fluency in these vital media is perceived to be out of touch with peoples' needs and is in danger of being bypassed for someone who "speaks their language." In addition to a top-rate and up-to-date website, the church should also have a Facebook page and a Twitter account. Try to enlist every member and attendee as a friend on Facebook. This is a great forum for sharing testimonies and good reports of things happening in the church, as well as keeping the congregation tuned in on upcoming events. Using Twitter to allow the members to track what their pastor is up to can really help people feel more intimately connected to you and the vision of the church. Rather than discourage the use of cell phones during services, some pastors encourage members to upload photos to Facebook or participate in a live opinion poll as part of their sermon. The opportunities for better communication and better church-building are limitless.

Remember – it's the message that's sacred, not the method!

4.4 INTRODUCING CHURCH GOVERNMENT

Most frictions or outright conflicts in church arise over the single question of authority – who's in charge? People tend to think that because they are spiritually mature, or have some spiritual insight, that they can override or ignore the authority of others they deem to be at a lower level. That may make sense in a strictly theological universe, but we are dealing with human beings here! And that always involves egos, personalities, emotional dynamics, and personal agendas. In order to get along we need to have a mutually agreeable organizational structure so that everyone knows their privileges and responsibilities towards the others. As has often been said, you can't build a church on structure alone, but neither can you build without it. So we need some type of workable system of government within churches in order to effectively pursue our goals and our vision together as a team.

Without a workable structure, communications get scrambled, lines of authority are not clear leading to frequent conflicts, people can't be held accountable, and things tend to get done through force of personality instead of good leadership. On top of that it's hard to measure any progress and many well-intended things just don't get done at all.

Most Pentecostal-type churches are not under-anointed – they are under-organized! There is a tendency to "wait on the Lord" to get things done. The problem here is that we often end up waiting on God to do what he has clearly told us to do. And then we attempt to do the work that is HIS and HIS alone to do! Sometimes we excuse our sloppy organization by claiming that we are just "staying open to the Holy Spirit". Never spiritualize your lack of preparation or diligence into openness to the Holy Spirit. God gives us vision and expects us to exercise all diligence in managing what he has put in our hands. You will always lose what you don't manage properly. (Matt 25:21) Moses needed both a burning bush AND a Jethro in order to succeed. In other words he needed both God's direction and skill in the day-to-day management of his people. Churches succeed when they have both a divine mandate and some management expertise. In other words, they need to focus not only on doing the right things, but also on doing things right.

Is there a biblical system of local church government? Not really. Paul's epistles mention some positional titles like elders, deacons, and bishops, but never really defines how they get appointed, what their duties are, or how long they would be in office. These are crucial questions in a functioning organizational structure. Instead, what we see are biblical principles of godly leadership that we must utilize in forming our structure, whatever shape it may take. This leaves the correct formula for church government somewhat fluid, flexible enough to adapt to a wide variety of eras and cultural settings, yet still reflect God's way of governing.

Whatever form we choose, effective church government must do three things:

1. Provide direction and organization.

2. Provide accountability for all involved.

3. Maintain morale and motivation.

Many different models have been employed by various church groups down through the history of the church. They range from dictatorial (senior leader is self-appointed and accountable to no one), Episcopalian (rule by a hierarchy of extra-local leaders), Presbyterian (rule by a council of local elders), and Congregational (everything is decided by congregational vote). Although all of these models utilize some biblical terminology, none of them are essentially 'biblical' models of church government. That doesn't mean that they are wrong or should be discarded. But because the New Testament isn't specific or emphatic about the internal structure of a church, we can assume that the overriding criteria is that it should be functional and effective. Historically, each of these schools of thought has assigned different meanings to such biblical terms as deacon or elder, making their definitions very ambiguous. We have found it helpful to just stick to functional titles. There is nothing ambiguous about titles like Worship Leader, or Head Usher, or Home Group Leader. Such a descriptive title sums up their responsibilities, the scope of their authority, and their term of office – all in one brief term. When a person no longer functions in a particular position, then they no longer carry the authority or responsibility that goes with it.

This is not the case with the designation of 'elder', which points to spiritual qualities rather than functional duties. And when there is a title given with no job description, no clear definition of authority, and no set term of office – in more cases than not, it is simply a recipe for conflict.

The guiding principles we see in the Bible are:

✓ Authority.

Because the universe we inhabit has an 'author', it is essentially authoritarian in nature. Ultimately God, as the Creator of all things, holds supreme authority. That is why the pot cannot say to the potter, "Why have you made me thus?" When people speak of having 'moral authority', they are actually appealing to the supreme court of morality – God. His authority then trickles down through those that he chooses to delegate it to: parents (Eph 6:1-2), spiritual leaders (Heb 13:17), and secular governmental leaders. (1 Tim 2:2, 1 Pet 2:13-14). So although all authority ultimately comes from God, within an organization it comes from those who give it to you. In a democracy, for example, when the voters vote you in, your authority comes from them. If you are then appointed by the head of the government to oversee the finance department, your authority comes from him. And that leads us to the next principle.

✓ Accountability.

Ultimately we are all accountable to God for our lives and everything that we have done. (2 Cor 5:10). But within an organization, accountability follows authority. In other words, we are accountable to whoever gave us the authority to lead. If the people voted you into office, then you are accountable to them and they have the right to direct you and the authority to vote you out too! If you were appointed to office by a bishop, for example, then only the bishop has the power to remove you or hold you accountable for your actions.

✓ Ability.

When someone has gained a degree of proficiency in a certain area, we say that they are an "authority in their field".

Others, who may in fact be over them in an organizational sense, will usually defer to their 'authority'. What this means to us in a church setting is that while we may staff positions with the best available candidate, ultimately we seek to place people into leadership positions according to their God-given gifting and its degree of development in their life.

Some are called to be primary leaders, others as secondary leaders, still others as helpers and supporters. (Matt 25:15, 1 Cor 12:28-30)

A further consideration regarding church government when it comes to church planting is that any model of formal church government will still have to be phased in over the first couple of years. You may have a particular model that you intend to utilize, but if you attempt to implement it too soon, it may even prove to be counter-productive to the new church. Like a newborn babe, you can't leave it in the hands of just anyone. Make sure leaders are proven and well-trained before you release them to lead. It's best to start with a provisional leadership structure, move to a transitional form, and finally, when everything is sufficiently ready, to your constitutional form. Here is what's involved in each phase:

> **A Simple, Workable System of Church Government**
>
> 1. Members
>   a. Application approved by the Board. Qualifications as set out in church bylaws
>   b. Responsible to vote, attend, tithe, and volunteer
>   c. Meet once a year for annual business meeting or as required
> 2. Directors/Board
>   d. Nominated by the pastor, voted into place by the members
>   e. Registered as incorporating directors with the government
>   f. Chaired by pastor, meets monthly or bi-monthly, or as needed
>   g. Responsible for legal and financial management, pastoral selection
> 3. Ministry Team
>   h. Staff, departmental, or various ministry leaders
>   i. Appointed and led by pastor, meets weekly
>   j. Responsible to plan, coordinate and oversee all other aspects of the church's work/ministry

Provisional

Throughout the first three years of a new church the leadership style must evolve from being quite autocratic to a highly participatory style. In a provisional phase of government the pastor/planter, out of necessity, makes virtually all decisions himself.

Since he is the one initiating the project, carrying the vision for it, and heading up whatever planting team is involved – he is the only one in a position to make most of the executive decisions.

These will typically involve deciding on a name and trademarks for the church, opening bank accounts, choosing facilities, purchasing AV equipment, assigning duties to team members, and so on. We always recommend having two arms-length individuals to sign cheques, for example. But in the early stages of a pioneer type church plant it just makes more sense for the planter to be the sole signatory.

In time he will have a trained leadership team to bounce decisions off of, but initially it's a bit of a one-man-show. This is simply a necessary reality, but at the same time he needs to begin training others for the leadership positions they will eventually fill. He should commence membership classes as soon as possible so that he can communicate the church's vision and leadership philosophy to new attendees.

This is the first step towards adopting a constitutional structure anyway. Organize people into short-term leadership positions and move them frequently. This enables you to assess their abilities and their faithfulness without giving them a place of influence in the church until they are ready. This phase may last for the first six months or longer.

Transitional

At this stage the pastor/planter still makes most decisions but should increasing consult with key departmental leaders before moving ahead with major decisions. This is important for helping to train upcoming leaders how to make sound decisions, but also to provide them a place to begin taking real ownership in the church. You want it to be 'their' church, not 'your' church! Continue to enlist people and train them in membership. The higher the ratio of members to attendees, the stronger the commitment level of the whole church will be. At this point it is a good idea to set up a planning team composed of departmental leaders to assist in planning services and events. The best individuals are usually those who have a call to full time ministry. Serving as departmental leaders and planning team members is part of the equipping process that may eventually see them released into a senior ministry position of their own. With so many programs and events of the church still in a developmental stage it is best to meet weekly with your planning team. Do a brief devotional or leadership teaching; review the past Sunday services, making notes of things to change or follow up on; go through the calendar of upcoming events to track their preparation and delegate responsibilities. You could also set up a visitation task force to carry out follow-up ministry and build fellowship. This also is a great equipping opportunity for future leaders. A third team you should form at this time is a finance committee to consult with and make financial reports to on a monthly basis.

Remember, none of these positions are formal at this point. These are people you appoint on a purely volunteer basis, but you will want to choose them based on their suitability for serving in these positions officially down the road a bit. In effect, you are training the people who will eventually serve as the church's staff, departmental leaders, and board members. This phase may last well into the third year of the church.

Constitutional

By the time the church approaches its third anniversary, if you have followed this process, you should have a strong base of committed members with a strong sense of shared vision and a good number of trained and proven leaders ready to step into formal leadership positions and serve. The church is now able to fully implement its constitutional government and by-laws. If you follow the simple government model outlined above then you should already have good people serving as your departmental leaders and/or staff. These people are appointed by the senior leader and as such are an extension of his ministry. The amount they are paid, if on a salary, will be set by the board, but the senior leader's prerogative is to select their own ministry team. The board, however, should be chosen and voted into office by the congregation. The pastor should have the right to screen nominations before any such vote, as he may be privy to information about them that other members may not. The kinds of individuals you want on your board are people who have a good track record in business leadership as well as a solid spiritual life. You are asking them to help guide the church and protect it legally and financially. That is why it may be best for you, as the senior leader, to nominate those who you know would be suitable candidates, and then put their names to a congregational ballot. Four or five board members on the board is ideal. Their names should be registered with the government as the legal board of directors. Give each one a portfolio such as facility management, finances, legal advisor, and train them to fulfill their roles with excellence. The result will be a church administration that consistently side-steps all the common pitfalls that a church can fall into. The better these things are managed, the more everyone can focus their energies on the spiritual life of the church.

4.6 CREATING A CHURCH CLIMATE THAT ATTRACTS LEADERS

You Can't Build A House Bigger Than It's Foundation

We can learn a lot from what Jesus did when He planted His Church on the day of Pentecost. 3,120 people on the first service. Jesus only let Peter have a one day crusade because there were only 120 trained committed leaders in place. Jesus had built a foundation that could handle 3,000 people and He knew that a house could not be built bigger than its foundation. When we plant churches, we have to plant them responsibly; but I believe what happened on the day of Pentecost can and will happen many, many times over all around the world in these last days.

On the day of Pentecost, Peter's message was aimed at reaching the Jews: proving to them that the resurrection of Christ was foretold in the Old Testament, and that Jesus was their promised Messiah. He also confronted them with their sin of crucifying the Prince of Life. When they heard these words, they were cut to the heart and asked, "What shall we do?" 3,000 souls repented, received Christ and were baptized in the name of Jesus. The preaching of God's Word releases great power! Preaching is truth on fire! Great preaching can change whole cities and nations.

The Bible determines the message, but our target determines when, where and how we communicate it. The message is sacred. The Word of God never changes. But our method must adapt to meet the needs of our target group. The strategies and programs are determined by the need, but the Bible is always the same.

Jesus targeted his ministry in order to be effective, not to be exclusive. We're not trying to exclude anybody from our church.

Everyone is welcome to come, but we need to have something to shoot at. Small churches become more effective when they specialize in what they do.

When you're first starting a church, you can't compete with the church down the street that has 15,000 members, millions of dollars, a great facility and every program you can think of in the church. You can't compete with it. Don't look at that giant and say, "I've got to do everything that they are doing," or you'll go crazy. You have to major on your strengths. There is one advantage that a small church has over a large church—it can be intimate and caring. The pastor can be touchable and know everyone by name. People are hungry for fellowship, friendship and intimacy. Build on your strengths and you will build an awesome church!

Attracting Leaders

Whether it's a local church or a church planting movement, we must be able to both train up leaders, and attract leaders who are already trained. If there are no new leaders a movement will eventually stop moving and die.

It took Jesus three years to find and develop 120 leaders. We will not be able to do it any quicker, but we can fast track some. Those closest to you will determine your level of success. David attracted leaders, Saul drove them away.

When David was a fugitive hiding in the cave of Adullam, 400 men joined themselves to David and made him their captain. These men were discontent, in debt and in distress. This has often been called the 3D Church. In time, David made great leaders out of many of these same men. It takes a leader to know a leader and it takes a leader to grow a leader (1 Samuel 22:1-2). Many years later after David had grown as a leader and a warrior the scripture says that mighty men of valour in their own right came and joined themselves unto David. These men had been trained in Saul's army but when Saul died they came and joined David (1 Chronicles 12:1, 8, 14, 17-18).

How can we create the kind of atmosphere that attracts mighty men of valour? What are leaders and potential leaders looking for?

Leaders and potential leaders will join you if:

1. They believe they can learn from you and grow under your ministry and in your church (Matthew 4:19). All leaders want to grow. It's hard to sit under someone who is a poor leader or someone who has stopped growing and you have already gone further than them. This is why you must keep on growing. As you keep growing the kind of leaders you will attract will get better. But when they do come don't be threatened or intimidated by them.

2. There is opportunity for promotion if they do grow. This is why it's important to have small groups and plant churches because they give leaders the opportunity to increase in their leadership skills. They can grow from being a leader of 5s to 10s, 50s, 100s, and 1000s according to the Exodus 18 principle. It's important to have a list of potential leaders and a list of potential positions available; the best way to do this and make it visible is by having a flow chart. As you pray over these lists and give thought to both the people and the positions, you'll be amazed how God will reveal where people fit best. Maximum fit, minimum stress.

3. Big vision attracts, builds, and releases big leaders. President De Gaulle said to Winston Churchill, "If you do big things you will attract big people; if you do little things you'll attract little people and little people will cause you lots of problems." Do things that are big enough to attract big people. We need to do some things that are big enough to attract media attention. We must have a vision and goals that are understandable; achievable and big enough to challenge the people. Leaders will ask themselves, "Is there room enough in this church and this movement for my calling and giftings?" Find out where your people are at and give them a challenge that will stretch them. "Attempt great things for God, expect great things from God" (William Carrey).

4. Leaders are attracted to an environment that is challenging, creative and flexible, along with order and good leadership. You must ask for commitment; if you don't you'll lose people, and if you do you'll lose people. It all depends on which group you want to keep and which group you want to lose.

If you ask for commitment, you'll keep the winners and lose the whiners. If you don't ask for commitment, you'll keep the whiners and lose the winners. The choice is yours, choose life!

Creating an environment that attracts leaders means:

- ✓ Having a clear vision and setting challenging, achievable goals
- ✓ Effectively sharing the vision and goals
- ✓ Actively pursuing the vision and fulfilling the goals
- ✓ Involving people in accomplishing set goals
- ✓ Finding out who is in your house, and matching them with appropriate responsibilities

In 2 Kings 4, the miracle of multiplication never stopped until they had no more empty pots to pour into. Gather as many potential leaders as you can and keep pouring into them. Keep wining souls and making disciples. Soul winning and discipleship comes out of relationship and leadership comes out of discipleship. What you are able to do is determined by who you have in your church.

You have to be willing to take a risk on people; a calculated risk. It is important for the people to believe in the leader, but it is more important that the leader believes in the people. Have a plan to prove people before you give them key areas of responsibility and a title. It's easy to set people into a position, but difficult to get them out! Hang around an experienced risk taker for a while. Barnabas was willing to help Paul when everyone else was afraid of him, because he saw potential in him and was willing to take a risk on him (Acts 9:26-27). We need to look for the good, believe the best and be willing to take a risk on people – because people are worth it! It has been said, "If your vision is for a year, plant wheat. If your vision is for ten years, plant trees. If your vision is for a lifetime, plant people." I would add, "If your vision is for eternity plant churches."

People are our greatest asset. To keep them we need to (John 10:1-5):

✓ Know them by name.

✓ Show them the way they must walk and the work they must do.

✓ Grow them by teaching and challenging them to obey God's word.

✓ Deploy them; thrust them forth as labourers into the harvest.

You have to create a positive atmosphere of faith and encouragement; one that makes it easier for people to believe God for big things. One that makes it easier for people to step out and take a risk, knowing that if they step out and fail, you'll still be there to pick them up, dust them off; and they will not be rejected.

What people can do is determined by their abilities and skills.

What they must do is determined by their passion and calling.

What they will do is determined by their surrender to the will of God.

Creating The Right Environment In Services

• The opening statements should inspire faith and create expectation. Oral Roberts' opening statement used to be, "Something good is going to happen." Kathryn Kuhlman would say, "I believe in miracles because I believe in God." They were both seeking to create an environment of expectation through faith in a good God.

✓ The songs you sing must be scriptural, uplifting and faith filled.

✓ The messages you preach must be relevant; practical; scriptural and faith-inspiring.

✓ The prayers you pray must be full of faith & encouragement.

✓ The life you live must be one that others can imitate, one that encourages them to live for Christ.

✓ The disposition of the upfront people in the church must be one that rises above discouragement and disappointment, confident in the knowledge that 'if God is for us who can be against us'. They must have a God Is Greater Than attitude!

All of these things can make a great difference to the spiritual climate in a church service. Let's set the spiritual temperature high and believe God for the miraculous! "Lord, I pray that you would encourage the apostles, prophets, evangelists, pastors and teachers to go on and grow on. That they may rise up to new levels of leadership and authority; so that the people in every sector of society would look once again to the church of the living God for answers to the problems of our day.

Help us to build and attract tomorrow's leaders today!"

Key questions that must be addressed:

✓ Are you planning to plant and set in another pastor?

✓ Are you planning to plant and be the long-term pastor?

If your job is to get the church established and then turn it over to someone else for long term leadership, then the responsibility for choosing the right leader may be largely yours. When looking for a pastor for a church, how do you find the right one? How do you know if you are the right pastor for a specific people or congregation? It is a bit like finding a marriage partner. The right choice can bring great success, but the wrong one can be a total disaster! One thing for sure, you are better off wanting what you don't have than having what you don't want. The following ideas will prove helpful in making a right choice.

1. The Courtship Period

Always try to arrange a courtship period so that you don't have to jump into this kind of a relationship too quickly. It's not enough to choose a pastor because he has preached two good messages. During the courtship period, both the congregation and the pastor will have a chance to observe one another and receive a confirmation one way or the other. When considering a partner for marriage we tell young people to go into it with eyes wide open and then afterwards keep your eyes half shut!

2. Does He Have A Love For The City And A Vision For The Area?

God won't call you somewhere that you don't love. A lot of missionaries go with a spirit of suspicion about the country where they are sent. They see and focus on the bad. Finally they get to the place where they become isolated from the very people they went to help. If you look for the good, believe the best and are willing to take a risk on people, you'll always find what you're looking for. With this kind of spirit and attitude you'll say, "I will trust you until you prove untrustworthy," rather than I won't trust you until you prove trustworthy.

A successful pastor must have this kind of spirit in order to receive a God-given vision for the area and have a long term love for the people and the City.

3. Does He Have A Love For The People And Can He Identify With Them?

What kinds of people live in the area? Is it a small town? Is it a rural community? Is there a university in the area? Or are you going to be dealing with street people? The pastor has to be able to love and identify with the people he seeks to reach.

4. Does He Have The Gifting And Ability Necessary To Meet The Needs Of The People And The Area?

It is necessary to match pastors up with the communities. Whether they come from within or from outside of the group, you have to make sure their personalities and gifting-mix line up with the city they are placed in. When a pastor comes from within the community he will be ministering in, it works against him at the beginning. "Oh, it's just old Bill. He's a farmer, not a preacher."

But after a period of time, it works for him. When he begins to succeed, the people's attitudes begin to change. "Wow! Look what Bill's done for the Lord! And, he's one of us! He's a great pastor! And, best of all, he understands us!"

5. Does He Have The Experience Necessary For The Task?

Can he handle the church at its present size and can he grow it? Jesus gave talents to each according to his own ability. This calls for some form of evaluation as to one's ability (Matthew 25:15). Of course we want to examine a candidate's track record and see what they've done and how well they've done it. But the past isn't always the best indicator of the future. People can go through a tough time, learn some great lessons, and go on to new levels of success. So you have to evaluate their past experience in the light of their character and their attitude towards their experience. Some people's experiences can leave them wounded and carrying a lot of baggage.

Others with much the same experience are energized by it and are living their lives with greater wisdom and direction than ever. We have to look at their past, then at their possible future; but it is where they are at the present that will determine whether or not they are ready to take on the lead role in the church and build a terrific future.

6. Does He Have A Servant Spirit?

He must look at leadership as a way to serve God and the people; not as a means to have power, control, money, position, prestige or an easy life. A person looking for authority will hurt you; a person looking for responsibility will bless you.

When I go to a church that needs a pastor, I firstly look to see if there's someone from within the church that has been raised up to possibly become the next pastor. If there is no one from within that church, then we'll send someone who has the call of God on their life from within our organization. This is much safer than bringing in someone from another organization, but it's still risky because there are going to be differences in the way the new pastor thinks and does things; and that can cause problems. The planter is unique in that all the people in the church have chosen to join him. His relationship with them is normally quite strong. But the incoming pastor has it the other way around – he is choosing to join the church. If he is wise he will come to his new position with the understanding that it will take time and good leadership for him to really win the trust and loyalty of the people.

When you're setting in a pastor, you always want to have the welfare of the people in mind. Transition is difficult, even in good times. There are things that a pastor who is releasing a church needs to understand; and there are things that the pastor who is receiving the church needs to understand.

After the new pastor has been set in, he will likely find that there will be people coming to him, and complaining about the last pastor. If he's not careful, he can hold resentment against the very man that released the church to him. If the new pastor picks up their offense, and begins to share some of this information with the rest of the congregation, those that loved the old pastor will get offended.

Things like this can split a church! Turning churches over is a delicate operation. You have to use wisdom to do it responsibly.

The ideal is to find and train leaders from within your church. But if the right person isn't in your congregation, then you still have to take the time to find the right kind of person to replace you so that you can leave responsibly, and your work remains and continues to grow after you have left. This is where a family of churches like Victory can be of major assistance in helping to assure pastoral release, divine placement and congregational stability.

We must train tomorrow's leaders - today

We must form tomorrow's teams - today

We must write tomorrow's books - today

We must compose tomorrow's music - today

We must buy tomorrow's properties - today

We must plant tomorrow's churches - today

We must develop tomorrow's programs and strategies - today

We must build tomorrow's structures - today

In this chapter we will discuss some of the pitfalls of church planting. There are a lot of things that can be avoided as you begin your new endeavor, and in so doing you can save yourself a lot of heartache and pain. Here are a number of things, gleaned from our experiences, which we have learned to avoid!

1. Starting a Church in the Wrong Place, at the Wrong Time, with the Wrong Leader

You can't make too many more mistakes than these. If you've missed God on even one of these elements, it can cause your church plant to fail.

If a good leader goes to the right place at the wrong time, he'll struggle. If you plant a church in the right place at the right time, but you've chosen the wrong leader, you're headed for trouble. If any one of these elements is out of place, it will make things difficult. But if you've missed it on all three, then you've got a disaster on your hands.

If you're moving in a particular direction and things aren't working out, you have to be flexible. In Acts 16, Paul was about to go down to Bithynia in Asia to preach the Gospel when the Lord spoke to him in the night and told him not to go. Here we see the right leader at the right time about to go to the wrong place.

God stopped him and showed him the right place. Thank God Paul was flexible enough to be able to change his course.

Instead of missing God, he immediately changed direction and went to Macedonia and planted the first church in Greece.

Sometimes we start moving in a particular direction, and as we're moving in that direction, we find out it's the wrong direction. We may be ready to plant a church. We may already know that its God's timing for us to step out and take on the role of a church planter. We may have the passion for it. But then, all of a sudden, God stops us and redirects us to another place. God will do that. In fact, it's not a difficult thing for Him to change your direction when you're headed somewhere.

2. Setting People Into Positions Too Soon

It's easy to put people into positions, but it's much more difficult to get them out if they're not right for the job. Unless you really know that you've got the right person and they have been faithful and proven over a period of time, don't put them in a position right away. Get them to commit to a temporary position, for three months. They may be like scaffolding on a building; they may be around to help you get your church off the ground, and then they'll move on.

A lot of people come in on the original church plant and are willing to do anything that is needed. So, you put them in charge of an area of ministry. But once the church begins to grow they no longer have the gifting necessary to take the area of ministry to where it needs to go. Now, if you've given them a position and a title, they may not want to turn it over to someone else with a stronger gifting. As a result, that whole area will suffer.

But if you can get them to make a three-month commitment, and communicate that to them right from the beginning, you can avoid a lot of problems. Let them know that at the end of three months they won't necessarily be considered the leader of that area. This way it will be much easier if you have to move them on to another area of ministry in order to make way for a more gifted individual.

3. Draining the Mother Church by Starting Too Many Churches, Too Soon

When I was the pastor of our first church in Calgary, I started several other churches very quickly. If I were to do it again, I might not start them as quickly as I did. But our church grew so fast. We were having four services on a Sunday, with three to five hundred people in each service. You can burn yourself out by preaching four times on a Sunday.

We looked for bigger facilities, but nothing opened up to us. We tried everything. But every time I put an offer on a building, it fell through. Buildings that sat on the market for years would sell two hours before I put in an offer, or we would find a building, but the city would not rezone it.

In some ways I was pressured to start those other churches. Looking back, I can see that was exactly God's plan. Sometimes the things that go wrong can make you more right. Some things that you struggle with will push you right into the will of God for your life. So, don't get frustrated and bent out of shape because things don't work exactly as you planned.

We released about 60 people to a Northeast Calgary church plant. Then we released two groups of people to a Southside Calgary church plant. Another 60 were sent to plant a downtown Calgary church. Forty-eight were released to plant a church in a smaller city just outside of Calgary called Airdrie, and then another 20 of my key leaders were released to pastor churches in other areas of Canada. In the end we released too many too quickly, and it became a major drain on the mother church. But we now have 15 great churches in and around the City of Calgary. God is a God of multiplication, and reproduction is the principle of life!

As soon as a church is birthed, it should get pregnant with another church. In fact, there is a cycle that churches need to go through, which is like a human cycle. There is the conception stage, the developing stage, the birthing stage, and then comes a time of growth, maturity, reproduction and death. That's the human life cycle, isn't it?

The same principle holds true in a local church or a ministry organization. First there's the conception. Many of you reading this book already have something birthed within your spirit. There's something developing within you pertaining to the birthing of a project God wants you to do!

Once a church has been birthed, it has to grow. We don't want to just birth babies; we want to birth healthy, hungry babies who will grow. Eventually, they will come to a place of maturity, where they are ready to reproduce. If they reach that stage of reproduction and don't reproduce, they will die. That's why 80,000 to 100,000 churches in North America closed their doors in the last decade of the 20th century. There are a lot of churches being planted, but most people don't realize that there are almost as many being closed down as are being planted.

I believe it's good for every local church to give birth to a daughter church within the first three to five years of their existence.

And then, once they've gained their strength back again, perhaps within two or three years, they should plant a second church. Sometimes when people get the church planting vision, they want to plant six new churches immediately. But you have to be careful not to drain the mother church too much, too soon. Otherwise, the mother church itself can shrivel up and die.

One of the devil's main strategies is to get us to reach for too much too soon; this causes us to be too weak to be effective in breaking through into new areas. We must work within our measure of rule, strengthen our present position and then reach out to plant new works from a position of strength and not weakness.

4. Wrong Church Government

Over the years we have been involved in putting a lot of churches back together after a church split. Out of all such churches not one had a proper church government. They were either set up as a one man operation or as a democracy where everyone had equal say. Neither system can work. When the pastor runs the entire church with very little communication, the church is off-balanced and the people are frustrated. When everyone has an equal say, the pastor really isn't the pastor. No one is leading.

Situations like these led us years ago to develop a stable and effective system of church government that is based on one man leadership with a system of checks and balances. These checks and balances have to be strong enough to bring accountability.

Of course when a church is first getting started, you have to implement a provisional type of church government that will allow the church to function, until you can set up proper church government.

5. Setting in a Pastor who is Unproven, Unprepared or in Rebellion

This is a faithful saying: if a man desires the position of a bishop, he desires a good work. A bishop then must be blameless, the husband of one wife, temperate, sober-minded, of good behaviour, hospitable, able to teach ....

Not a novice, lest being lifted up with pride he fall into the condemnation of the devil. (1 Timothy 3:1-2, 6, emphasis added)

In this passage, Paul says that a pastor must not be a novice. Rather, he must be an individual who has been prepared and proven. We require that he be proven through working in a small group or running an area in the local church. He must have been faithful in that which is another man's before the Lord will trust him with that which is his own. His marriage, finances and character must be in good order.

There have been some people that I wasn't able to put into ministry simply because of their financial condition. They were so far in debt that it took them an astronomical amount of money just to live.

So, one of the things I always ask when I'm hiring a pastor is, "What's the least you can live on?" I don't ask that question because that's what I intend to pay them. I want to know if they have been able to fine tune their finances.

Some people don't know how to handle money. They waste money and ring up a lot of credit card debt. If that's what they do with their own finances, how are they going to run the church? Sometimes we set people in the ministry too soon. Just because they want to be in the ministry doesn't mean you should release them into it. Some people are just not ready.

6. Poor Communication and No Accountability

When a church first starts, the pastor has to have regular meetings with a group of potential leaders in the church. I have seen some pastors who don't communicate with anyone in the church.

Since the people have no input, they get frustrated and leave. Good leaders draw contributions from both those under them and those over them. Better to succeed as a team-player than fail as a superman.

Any one of these pitfalls can sabotage your church plant. Do your best to avoid them.

4.9 CHARACTERISTICS OF UNSUCCESSFUL CHURCH PLANTS

The following statistics are the results of a survey by Todd Hunter .

This is a church plant autopsy report. These characteristics give us valuable insight into why these churches failed. The results are based on telephone conversations with 22 pastors of failed plants. The interviewer, Todd Hunter, had either supervised these pastors (or knew them personally) and could, in most instances, agree with the pastors' evaluations. The number in parenthesis represents the percentage of pastors who mentioned that particular problem.

1. Inability to Identify, Recruit, Train and Deploy Workers and Leaders (95%)

It's amazing how many people are weak in this area. As pastors, we have to be able to see diamonds in the rough. We have to be able to see the diamond when it's just a lump of coal. That's all a diamond is, a lump of coal that's been under pressure for a long time. A good leader is able to see under the surface and beyond the obvious.

Then, not only do you have to be able to find potential leaders, you must also be able to train them and release them into areas of ministry. Without this skill, a church plant is destined to fail.

2. Ineffective Evangelism and an Unwillingness to be Ruthless in Evaluations (77%)

Churches are built on evangelism. You have to get out on the streets! Go door to door! Visit people, talk to them, and love them! Without a focus on evangelism, your church is not going to grow. If something is not working, you have to be able to swallow your pride, admit your mistakes, and start again with a new plan and fresh enthusiasm.

3. No Clear Vision (77%)

A lack of clear vision results in working hard at the wrong things. A church planter has to be able to focus his energy. It's amazing what you can do once you get focused on a vision, and then channel all of your energies into that focus.

One way the Devil can destroy your future is to fragment your focus. He will get you focused on so many things that you deplete your energies without having ever been effective at anything.

4. Problems With Supervision and/or Authority (73%)

A lot of people in our day neither understand nor accept spiritual authority. This is a good subject to teach in the early days of a church plant. People need to learn how to respond to authority. Then, teach on the areas of delegation, motivation, supervision and coordination. You will save yourself hours of unnecessary counselling time.

5. The Pastor was a Nurturer and Father, rather than an Aggressive Leader and Equipper (68%)

There is a difference between a nurturer and an enabler. A nurturer is more of a counsellor. He usually has a mercy motivation. He can sit in his office all day while hurting people come to him for counsel and advice. But, the key man in a church plant needs to be an assertive leader and an equipper. He may have a few nurturers who work with him, but he needs to be a leader.

6. The Pastor was Unwilling to Take Responsibility for Church Growth (65%)

If the church is not growing, the buck comes back to the senior man. If I'm the senior man, I have to assume responsibility for growth in my church. A lot of pastors are not willing to accept that responsibility. They would rather blame the lack of growth on various circumstances, and that may be part of the problem. But as the senior man, you must be responsible for finding solutions to the problems, so the church can move ahead and grow.

7. Self-Image Problems in the Pastor or Key People (55%)

Their self-image is either too low or too high. They have either a poor self-image, or an over-inflated ego, both of which will eventually cause a church plant to fail.

8. The Pastor Is Unsure of His Calling (50%)

If you know that you're a church planter and you know that you're doing what God has called you to do, you will have a much greater sense of confidence. You will stand even in the midst of opposition because you know that this is what you're called to do. Somehow, someway, God is going to bring you through and bless you.

Some of the other characteristics that were mentioned were: Failure to research and understand community demographics (64%), no extra-local support and encouragement from other leaders and churches (64%), the pastor was unsure about the Holy Spirit's leading and ministry (59%).

✓ Describe your follow-up plan to bring Launch Day visitors back again.

_____

_____

_____

_____

_____

✓ How do you plan to continue making new contacts in the community following your launch?

_____

_____

_____

_____

_____

✓ Do you have a full slate of programs planned that will give people multiple ways to plug in? What are they and who will lead them?

_____

_____

_____

_____

_____

✓ Are you planning to plant and pastor long term? Or get the church established and set in another pastor? If so, how will this affect the way you lead the church?

_____

_____

_____

_____

_____

✓ Do you have a membership course ready to teach? Does it cover the model of church government that the church will eventually utilize?

_____

_____

_____

_____

_____

SECTION 5
Time To Get Started

So, at last you're ready to go! You're the right person for the job. You've got the right team around you. You're confident that you have God's plan and God's timing. You've prayerfully mapped out your vision, your launch strategy, and your follow-up plans. Now what?

Ensuring Prayer Support

As much as we have focused in this book on the mechanics and strategies of getting new churches launched, it goes without saying that "unless the Lord builds the house, they labour in vain who build it." Nothing is built to last for eternity unless it is built upon a foundation of prayer: prayer that seeks God, hears from God, obeys God, and ignites faith in God.

Make no mistake – church planting is front-line spiritual warfare! It is nothing less than marching boldly into enemy territory and stealing his goods right from under his nose! Successfully done, it sets captives free, breaks demonic strongholds over individuals and families, and shakes the grip of spiritual principalities over whole cities. If believers aren't aware that all this is going on when they set out to plant a new church – the enemy certainly is! And he doesn't like it a bit. Unless the planter, his family, team, and whole project are bathed in prayer, they leave themselves wide open to his counter-attacks. The sad fact is that many have set out to establish a new work for the glory of God – only to end a year later disgraced, financially ruined, and their family gone. This is a devastating tragedy for the whole body of Christ, and one that is totally avoidable if we only birth the church in prayer and keep our spiritual armour on!

The first priority of prayer is for the planter himself. Only in the private place of prayer can he ensure that his heart is free from selfish, ego-driven motives; that his spiritual walk is strong and consistent, his lifestyle holy, and his house in order. He needs to cultivate an attitude of confident faith that flows from a heart-conviction of God's leading and God's favour on the plant. He will need to resist discouragement, overcome insurmountable challenges, and stare down opposition of all kinds. If he isn't a man of prayer then he'd better have a mother who is!

Secondly, you need prayer to make sure that you have the Lord's leading in the project. Those who talk to God the most are the ones who hear from God the most. Long before final decisions are made to begin the planting process, the leader, his family, and other key leaders need to know that they have God's man and God's plan. It is essential that a husband and wife ministry team have an agreement in prayer before they move forward. If they start out that way, then the pressures and challenges along the way will only drive them closer together. Seek the input of trusted spiritual leaders and ask them to seek God about it before you commit to the plant.

Thirdly, pray in the right team. Most of the problems you encounter in the first six months of a new church originate from within the original planting team. Long term relationship can help to prevent sudden changes in people's lives, but only the leading of the Holy Spirit can insure that you have the right people around you when you need them to be. The last thing you need when some spiritual maverick shows up and challenges your leadership, is for someone on your own team to side with them and help lead a church split! You need the mind of Christ not only in selecting the right team members, but in leading and relating to them as well. Your success will be determined by those that are closest to you, so pray them successful too! You are the pastor to your team before you have to pastor any new members. Hold them up in prayer and they will be the right team through thick and thin.

Fourthly, you need to pray for God to provide. Most church plants are carried off on a very limited budget and a lot of faith! God loves church planting and delights to show himself as your Provider. It is not uncommon for totally unsaved strangers to walk in at a crucial moment, make a huge cash donation, walk out and never be heard from again! In one of our church plants there was a man in the community having trouble with his teenaged daughter. When he heard that our church had a good program going for youth, he came by and gave a $10,000 donation for sound equipment. He never did attend one service! There are so many things that a new church needs to acquire, all at a time when its giving levels are probably at the lowest point they will ever be. But as the team prays for these needs to be met, God makes a way.

He has amazing ways to supply everything from a deal on sound equipment to a miracle facility at the last possible moment. Even when you have all the promised support you think you will need, pray for God's provision and favour with the community. Often community people who respond to a need in the church plant end up on the front row with their whole family!

And last but not least, planting churches is all about reaching the lost and enlarging the kingdom of God – pray for souls. Pray for those God has pre-ordained to belong to your church to find their way there. Pray for the salvation of civic leaders and politicians. Pray for opportunities to reach the students in the schools. Pray for key business people to get saved and add their influence to the growing church. Pray for family and extended family of every new attender. Go door to door and offer to pray for the neighbours around the church's meeting place. Pray against false religious strongholds over the area, against spirits of addiction, family violence, and complacency that hold many spiritually captive. Identify the spiritual strongholds over your city and wage war on them until there is an open heaven over the whole region. Pray that God would empower you and your people to reach every available person, by every available means, and at every available time with the Gospel of Jesus Christ!

www.ingramcontent.com/pod-product-compliance
Lightning Source LLC
Chambersburg PA
CBHW070806100426
42742CB00012B/2271